2

Understanding
Of Mice and Men,
The Red Pony,
and *The Pearl*

The Greenwood Press "Literature in Context" Series

Understanding *To Kill a Mockingbird*: A Student Casebook to Issues, Sources, and Historic Documents
Claudia Durst Johnson

Understanding *The Scarlet Letter*: A Student Casebook to Issues, Sources, and Historical Documents
Claudia Durst Johnson

Understanding *Adventures of Huckleberry Finn*: A Student Casebook to Issues, Sources, and Historical Documents
Claudia Durst Johnson

Understanding *Macbeth*: A Student Casebook to Issues, Sources, and Historical Documents
Faith Nostbakken

Understanding Shakespeare's *Julius Caesar*: A Student Casebook to Issues, Sources, and Historical Documents
Thomas Derrick

UNDERSTANDING
Of Mice and Men,
The Red Pony,
and *The Pearl*

A STUDENT CASEBOOK TO ISSUES, SOURCES, AND HISTORICAL DOCUMENTS

Claudia Durst Johnson

The Greenwood Press
"Literature in Context" Series

GREENWOOD PRESS
Westport, Connecticut • London

Library of Congress Cataloging-in-Publication Data

Johnson, Claudia D.
    Understanding Of mice and men, The red pony, and The pearl : a
student casebook to issues, sources, and historical documents /
Claudia Durst Johnson.
        p.   cm. — (The Greenwood Press "Literature in context"
series, ISSN 1074–598X)
    Includes bibliographical references and index.
    ISBN 0–313–29966–8 (alk. paper)
    1. Steinbeck, John, 1902–1968. Of mice and men.   2. Steinbeck,
John, 1902–1968. Red pony.   3. Steinbeck, John, 1902–1968. Pearl.
I. Title. II. Series.
PS3537.T32340464   1997
813'.52—dc20   96–41332

British Library Cataloguing in Publication Data is available.

Library of Congress Catalog Card Number: 96–41332
ISBN: 0–313–29966–8
ISSN: 1074–598X

First published in 1997

Greenwood Press, 88 Post Road West, Westport, CT 06881
An imprint of Greenwood Publishing Group, Inc.

Printed in the United States of America

The paper used in this book complies with the
Permanent Paper Standard issued by the National
Information Standards Organization (Z39.48–1984).

10 9 8 7 6 5 4 3 2

Contents

Introduction

The three novellas by John Steinbeck that are the subject of this study have several things in common. All are set in the far western part of the New World far from the influences of the New England and Virginia cultures that shaped the East. Two are set in California and one in Mexico. All three novellas have dramatic structures and have been dramatized on stage or screen. And all are among the most frequently read texts in secondary schools in both Great Britain and America.

Like John Steinbeck's most famous novel, *The Grapes of Wrath*, these three novellas are rich in contextual references to the history of California and Mexico and to issues vital and peculiar to their settings. Consequently, the background against which each is set is important to a full understanding of the work, and these works of fiction are, as well, a window on the history of the times.

Although he incorporated universal themes into his fiction, Steinbeck is considered a regional writer. Most of his novels and short stories take place in the area around Monterey, California, where he grew up, a region culturally distinct from the Midwest, South, and Northeast. It was still frontier and still unknown to English-speaking settlers some two hundred years after the English settled Massachusetts. One major context in which *The Red Pony* must be placed is the early history of California, for its characters lived within seventy years of the first settlement of the area by English-speaking people.

In addition to the nineteenth-century history of California, another important context, especially for *Of Mice and Men*, is the first two decades of the twentieth century, when agriculture and land use in California began to take on a special character and the difficulties of farm laborers in the state foreshadowed problems that would spread throughout the whole nation in the Great Depression of the 1930s.

The setting of the third novella, *The Pearl*, is Mexico in the early years of the twentieth century, when the plight of the peasants, particularly the Indians native to Mexico, bred anger and continual revolution.

Steinbeck is also considered to be a social/political commentator, especially on the plight of the migrant worker in the Great Depression. At one time in the 1930s California agricultural associations called John Steinbeck the most dangerous man in America because of his support of the lowly farm worker. All three of these novellas deal with social issues of the elderly poor, the migrant, members of oppressed races, and powerless people in general who are at the mercy of a cold or greedy society.

Chapter 1 is a study of key literary themes common to all three novellas. Among these are the unfailing aspirations of even the lowliest, least powerful character to be a greater person or to have a better life, and the influence on humans of the powerful forces of nature, which operate for both good and ill.

Subsequent chapters place these three novellas in context, exploring the historical background and raising the enduring issues implicit in the works. Chapter 2, which is the first contextual one, is called "Old California and the West." For many of Steinbeck's characters, California represented a dream of Eden—a place where they would flourish as never before possible. Here we read accounts of eighteenth- and nineteenth-century travelers who dreamed of a land of milk and honey. Chapter 3 presents selections on the meaning of land ownership—the great draw of the New World and then of the West—and the corruption of the ideal of land ownership. Chapter 4 focuses on the single male worker in California history whose life is spent on the move and without a family. Chapter 5 looks more specifically at the problems of being homeless and hopeless in the country that was supposed to be the land of plenty. The final chapter is on the oppression of the poor in Mexico (based on rigid class and race divisions), which provoked a century of revolutions.

Documents include reports of United States government commissions, memoirs of mountain men and pioneers, books of travel, sociological studies, a political treatise, a journal, a comic memoir, and a new interview.

Topics for written or oral exploration and suggestions for further reading end each chapter.

Page numbers refer to the Penguin Books editions of Steinbeck's three novellas.

"The Triumph of Our Species": A Literary Analysis of Three Steinbeck Novellas

In John Steinbeck's *The Red Pony*, the young boy Jody faces a flock of buzzards, one of which has already begun to devour the eye of a pet pony. In *Of Mice and Men* one drifter tells another of his plans for the two of them to own a farm. In *The Pearl* a young father defies community leaders in pursuit of a plan to send his son to school. These striking images from three novellas are clues to the range of both Steinbeck's style and philosophical concerns. In the first instance, we see stark nature—brutal, hideous, powerfully destructive. In the second and third we see the power of the human spirit to dream.

These three popular novellas show the dual, sometimes contradictory approaches found in Steinbeck's work. The first might be called the power of nature in the raw; the second, the struggle of humans to rise above nature and a naturalistic society.

That the idea of nature should assume such an important place in Steinbeck's work is not surprising. He was trained by his closest friend, Ed Ricketts, to be a natural scientist. Steinbeck spent many hours of his adult life in a laboratory in Monterey, California, where Ricketts taught him a scientific method of general observation as well as a specific method for studying marine life in the laboratory. Steinbeck helped Ricketts in his experiments, work that culminated in a series of scientific expeditions which they recounted in *The Sea of Cortez,* published in 1941. Ricketts even appears as different characters in Steinbeck's fiction.

Steinbeck's knowledge of the natural world becomes evident in a number of ways: through his delineation of landscape as if it were itself a character with power over the lives of the human characters; through his description of the power of nature to shape society in its cruel image; through his use of animals as elements in his plots and as a critical part of his imagery; and in his characterization of nature as an all-powerful force against which people must struggle with only their dreams as weapons. These three novellas, despite their different settings—a family-run ranch, a workers' bunkhouse, and a poor community in Mexico—and their diverse main characters—a young boy, two drifters, and a Mexican peasant—share a common theme: the possibility of the human species to rise above base nature.

THE RED PONY: "THE GIFT"

The first of the four stories in *The Red Pony,* "The Gift," is essentially about the changing interaction of humans with the natural world. It is a mythic story of the Garden of Eden played out on a California farm by a ten-year-old boy who is expelled from the happy innocence of his childhood Paradise. As such, of course, it is also a story of initiation into the harsh reality of the adult world.

We will examine three aspects of this story of man and nature. First we look at Jody and his interaction with people and nature before the changes in his life begin, observing his own character, how he sees the landscape and animals with which he seems to be in union, his mother and father, and Billy Buck, the man who looms so large in his life as an all-knowing mentor and father figure. The second major aspect is the pony itself as a means to learning, action, and engagement. Finally we look at what might be called "the fall," or the immense change in the boy's relationship to nature by the end of the story: the changes in Jody himself, in how he reacts to the brutal naturalism he confronts, the changes in how he sees his idol, Billy, and the role Carl Tiflin plays in Jody's encounter with brute nature.

The title, "The Gift," has multiple meanings. The red pony is, of course, a gift for Jody. But the title is also ironic, for in the end this gift is the means through which Jody experiences a shattering confrontation with the suffering and callousness of the real world where nature reigns. It is a gift of death.

Jody, as a young boy who first receives the gift of a pony, is a somewhat carefree only child on the farm (often called a ranch in California) which his parents run with the help of Billy Buck. A shy, quiet, passive child who observes and listens rather than acts, Jody follows the orders of his elders. In the first scene, he knows from listening to the sounds near the kitchen door that his father is not wearing boots. He is even sensitive to the tones he hears in adult voices, for example, feeling pleased when he smells brandy on his father's breath, since he has learned that at such times his father is more mellow and sociable. He knows from the sounds in the kitchen late at night that some joke is afoot, and he is alert to his father's tone of voice (which makes him slightly uncomfortable) when Jody is ordered to follow him on the morning he receives the pony.

Jody also observes the landscape itself as well as adults. On the first morning, before he receives his gift, he makes the rounds of the ranch, observing the dogs, then the chickens as he walks by their pen, the green corn and the cow pumpkins in the vegetable garden, the sagebrush line at the edge of cultivation, and the tub he likes to drink from. His habit as an observer is underscored in this scene as he looks down on the ranch.

While Jody observes, he does not act on his own. The routines of his life are dictated by his father and mother. When the triangle is rung for wake-up in the morning, "it didn't occur to him to disobey the harsh note. He never had: no one he knew ever had" (2). Jody obeys his father in all things.

Jody's playground is the ranch itself. Like Adam and Eve in the Garden of Eden, he is surrounded by its animals—the tame dogs, pigs, chickens, and horses, and the wild quail, coyote, mice, and birds that live on the periphery of the yard. In the world of the ranch, even before Jody receives his pony, he is taught by animals. Like Adam, he is the prince of his domain, the one seemingly in control of the lower animals around him. The dogs follow him, the chickens and quail are fed by him, the pony depends on him utterly, and the pigs are slaughtered with his help.

From Jody's perspective on that first morning when his father and Billy leave the ranch, there is for him a feeling of comfortable unity, a soothing certainty in the landscape and among the animals who inhabit it. Yet, ironically, all around him are signs of nature's brutality—of the truth that in nature everything is a killer and devourer. The mission undertaken by Billy and his father on this day, as Jody well knows, is a mission of death; they take all the old cows to the butcher to be slaughtered. In a brutal contest, one of his two dogs has killed a coyote who had ripped off his ear. He has knowledge of the hoot owls hunting mice, hawks and blackbirds fighting for food and survival, and ticks sucking the blood of the dogs.

Throughout the story, he is constantly reminded of the slaughter and consumption of pigs by humans. On the first morning of the story, he passes the black kettle under the cypress tree "where the pigs were scalded" (4), and believes that his father demands his help to kill a pig on the morning that he is first introduced to the red pony. Though that is not the business planned for the day, he again passes the cypress tree, "where a singletree hung from a limb to butcher the pigs on" (8). Also on the first morning of his story, Jody coolly observes the buzzards flying low and knows that it means an animal has died somewhere near by. All these hints of death and devouring portend the gory climax of "The Gift." But at the story's beginning, Jody accepts death disinterestedly as an everyday fact of life. He *observes* it, but he has not *experienced* it. His senses and intellect have been engaged with death, but not his heart and feelings. In this sense, when the story opens, he is in a state of innocence (here meaning ignorance) of life's—that is, nature's—cruel realities.

Jody's father, Carl, might be seen to represent the harsher elements of nature in human form. Darwinian in his belief in the survival of the fittest, Carl is a suppressor of what he sees as weakness. To weed out weakness, much as strong animals attack weak ones of the same species, Carl uses an absolute and strict form of discipline. He is used to giving orders. He is introduced in the story as a "disciplinarian" (3), and in the name of "good discipline" attaches strings to any gifts he gives—like the rifle he has presented to Jody (7). The reader finds that the effect of his attitude is to keep Jody in a constant state of apprehension around his father. The result is fear, creating "a kind of doom in the air" (8). Rarely does Jody find any warmth in his father that lifts him beyond the somewhat cold and persistent necessity, found in harshest nature, to weed out weakness. But even the funny stories he tells to get Jody's mind off the sick pony are poetically self-revealing: like the Maxwell brothers who lost a vein of gold in the story Carl tells, he has also lost a streak of potential humanity in himself—the gold that represents innocence and purity. Like the wild man he describes, who has the ears and tail of a horse, Carl has become less human over the years in his need to survive. And like the rabbit-cats who hop into trees to capture birds, he is essentially a grotesque—scarcely human in his identification with the harshest elements of nature—one who fights to devour in order to survive.

Billy Buck, while he is in tune with the landscape and the animals on the ranch, is more fully human than Jody's father. Billy seems to know everything. He's the one who tells Jody where the pony came from, the one who makes the hair rope for Billy and tells him the secrets of raising a colt. Jody listens to him because Billy has a county-wide reputation of being excellent with horses, who "nearly always won first prize at the stock trials" (15). And Jody's mother tells him that Billy is "as good as any horse doctor in the country" (24).

Yet Billy has the compassion and feeling and humor of human nature that Jody's father seems to have only in very short supply. When Carl leads his son to the pony for the first time, his natural response is to deliver a threat with the gift—"If I ever hear of you not feeding him or leaving his stall dirty, I'll sell him in a minute" (9)—and then to leave in embarrassment at having been "soft" and giving. Billy's response is to offer help and information, and to laugh easily and with affection. When the pony becomes sick, Billy uses all his knowledge in an effort to make the animal well, while Carl either grouses about "weakness put into animals and men" by too much coddling (23) or hides the concern he has for Jody, inappropriately trying to divert him with funny stories. Even after Billy has profoundly disappointed Jody, he still reveals his understanding human spirit, the empathy that the boy's father seems to lack.

For these reasons, Billy Buck has become Jody's idol. It is easier for Jody to talk to Billy Buck (9). And Billy inspires admiration, trust, and confidence in the young boy. He is the epitome of "the man on the horse" who is "spiritually as well as physically bigger than a man on foot" (11). That is, he is one with nature, and at the same time is spiritually superior to brute nature.

But Billy Buck has a flaw. He tends to romanticize and to have too much faith in his own ability to keep nature under control. In telling Jody all he knows about horses, Billy attributes human qualities to them. Billy is also convinced that horses understand much more than simple commands—that they can comprehend explanations of events. Moreover, Billy's experience has led him to believe that animals and natural events can be controlled.

The gift of the pony accelerates Jody's inevitable initiation into the real world, a world where heroes show themselves to be flawed, where nature is brutal, and where death intrudes. Even before the pony arrives on the scene, Jody's innocent world is beginning to be threatened. He is feeling the approach of death, unavoidable in the fall of the year as he begins school, sensing that some drastic change is at hand. And the death that will eventually come home to him and will be deeply felt by him is foreshadowed by the "two big black buzzards" in search of a dead animal—a sight he notes on the day Billy and his father go to town to buy the pony.

After the pony arrives, there is an immense change in Jody externally. Once a passive observer on the ranch, he becomes active, learning how to take responsibility for Gabilan, the pony. Traditionally, boys in many societies, including the Native American culture, had mentors or teachers to assist them through their initiation into adulthood; Billy Buck is such a mentor for Jody. But while the older man offers information and support, Jody must now actually carry through with the training of the pony. He has the sole responsibility for feeding, grooming, exercising, halter-breaking, and finally training him to the saddle to be ridden.

As Jody becomes more active than passive, he feels more intensely than ever that things are changing and that he is on a journey of initiation. The very presence of Gabilan and Jody's new role as his owner make the world seem markedly different. Curiously enough, even on the morning before his father presents him with the pony, he had a sense of foreboding. Now in the midst of his happiness with the pony, he has an uneasy feeling that the result of the alteration, the end of the journey, will be disastrous. Something inside him tries to prepare him as he envisions the disappearance of Gabilan.

A change occurs in Jody's relationship to the natural world in which he has always lived, especially in his new sense of nature's inevitability—death—which has always been around him but somehow never touched him. In one scene, described in the midst of Gabilan's sickness, Jody feels that even the natural landscape itself has changed.

The reader knows, however, that the change has occurred not in the landscape, but in Jody. As Gabilan's condition worsens, the inevitability of death approaches, drawing Jody out of his childlike innocence into the harsh reality of the adult world. It can be seen in the movement of the story from a romantic rural idyll of a child on a farm to a ghastly tale of the brutality of nature, described with naturalistic, unsparing detail. As the condition of the pony worsens, so does the horror. At first the pony is described as having mucus stuck in his eyes and fluid running from his nostrils. The next day Jody watches as Billy slashes the pony's throat and yellow pus bursts out.

At the end, the naturalistic detail becomes almost too brutal to read. Jody experiences the reality of nature as he sees it represented in the buzzard itself—devouring, dumb, and death-filled. The naturalistic philosophy has engulfed "The Gift": he is utterly helpless to stop a blind and horrifying force of nature. In beating the bird's head into "a red pulp," Jody seems not only to be reacting to the death and devouring that is a part of nature (he has just killed a tick that was feeding on the dog and has heard the owls shrieking in the hayloft as they hunt for mice to eat), but also defying brute nature's unfeeling, impersonal acceptance of its own cruelty.

Part of his dejection, as he turns home at the end, comes from his sense that the journey to experience is a realization that man and nature, the boy and the pony, are not one and the same. Like Billy Buck, Jody has repeatedly humanized the pony, giving it human attributes. In death, Gabilan belongs to another world entirely.

In the course of Jody's coming of age, he must confront the downfall of his idol, Billy Buck, who nevertheless is presented favorably, in contrast to Jody's father, Carl Tiflin. The very name, "Billy," suggests that the hired man, for all his expertise, has some of the innocent spirit of a boy. Billy has acted as Jody's mentor at each stage in training the pony, but his downfall as the perfect, wise, all-knowing father-substitute begins when he talks Jody out of keeping Gabilan in the barn, predicts that it will not rain, and fails to get home in time to bring the pony in out of the rain as he had promised to do. The second stage of his failure comes when he tells Jody that the rain won't hurt the animal. The third stage occurs when he assures Jody that he can make the pony well again.

Although the romantic figure of Billy Buck is found to be flawed, in contrast with Jody's father he displays a finer human spirit that lifts him above the dog-eat-dog, devouring nature represented by the buzzard. Billy has a great heart—a sensitivity—that allows him to feel Jody's pain and recognize his spiritual need to remain all night by the pony's side. Like Jody himself, Billy is full of feeling when the pony dies, carrying the boy back to the house in his arms and lashing out at Carl Tiflin, who, like the buzzard, seems to have little imagination and feeling for the wounded boy, thinking that Jody has killed the buzzard because he mistakenly believes the bird has actually killed the pony. In the slang of the 1990s, Carl Tiflin hasn't a clue.

Finally, while the story attests to a hard truth about the cruelty of brute nature, it also affirms the possibility of a finer human spirit that brings feeling and imagination to bear upon the world, causing pain but also lifting some human beings above the devouring world.

THE RED PONY: "THE GREAT MOUNTAINS"

Like "The Gift," the second story in *The Red Pony*, "The Great Mountains," is constructed around a contrast between two different views of life. While in "The Gift" the brute force of nature is opposed to a finer human sensibility, in "The Great Mountains" religious meaning (very broadly speaking) is placed in opposition to the materialism and practicality of everyday life. As before, Carl Tiflin represents the limited vision of one who advocates the latter. His opposite is the old paisano (a Spanish American peasant) named Gitano.

The story opens with Jody mindlessly engaged in baseness and senseless cruelty. As if life has no meaning and he has nothing to do, he "listlessly" throws rocks to destroy all the swallows' nests around the barn and sets a trap with cheese in order to hurt the dog. He throws a rock at the dog for no reason at all and then proceeds to kill a bird with his slingshot, afterwards cutting it into pieces. These senseless cruelties attest to a vacancy in his life.

Yet Jody seems to yearn for meaning, for, following on these destructive acts proceeding from emptiness and boredom, he stares at what embodies divinity in the story—the great mountains, called the Great Ones, which he can see to the west of the ranch. Godlike in their mystery and immensity, these mountains have become an obsession with him, and he keeps asking everyone around him—mother, father, and Billy Buck—what lies in the mountains and if they have ever visited them. Jody's fascination and questions are not just about mountains; they are about what the mountains represent—the great mystery of the world, the meaning of life that goes beyond mere physical survival, perhaps even God.

Of the three people he queries, it is, not unexpectedly, his down-to-earth father who is most emphatic in insisting that "there's nothing there" (41). But Jody "knows different." He senses that there is a reality of the spirit that cannot be measured with the five senses.

The initiating incident in the story—that which sets the rest of the action in motion—is the appearance of the old man Gitano. He is mystical rather than materialistic in sentiment; his actions are guided not by reason and the five senses, but by deep and ancient feelings. He appears mysteriously from out of nowhere and as mysteriously disappears. He inexplicably announces that he has come back to the place where he was born and repeatedly insists that he will stay until he dies, even though there is no explanation for why he must do this and no hope that he can actually stay.

Gitano carries a deerskin and a rapier like magical totems, cherished religious and traditional relics. Jody recognizes that the old man and his relics are part of some kind of spiritual truth to which he is drawn.

Gitano's identification with the spiritual rather than the material, practical world is also found in his connection with the Great Mountains. Like them, he is deep, unknowable, and mysterious. Unlike most people, he has actually visited the mountains and, at the end, disappears heading toward them. Jody recognizes something sympathetic between the two, realizing that he is attracted to the old man just as he is pulled toward the mountains. Gitano is also identified with old Easter, the horse who has outlived his usefulness on this earth, as Gitano has himself.

From the moment Gitano arrives, his spirit uplifted toward the mountains, he seems one with God, or at least something higher than the natural, physical world of the ranch. His nemesis is Carl Tiflin, the practical man who places value on animals and people according to their ability to work and help make the ranch successful. Carl belittles as "soft" everything that the old man represents. He is angered by Gitano's quiet insistence that he will stay at the ranch and do small jobs, angered by the sympathy that others in the family show toward the old man. Sensing full well the parallels between old Easter and Gitano, Carl turns cruel, announcing, "Old things ought to be put out of their misery. . . . [H]e ought to be shot now" (48, 49).

Carl's cruelty further links Gitano, the old man, with Jody, the young boy: when Carl probes "for a place to hurt in Gitano," Jody is reminded that he himself has often been hurt by his father.

Carl is so absorbed in the physical business of running the ranch that his vision is limited and he is completely insensitive to things other than earth-bound, businesslike practicalities. He has no inkling, as the others do, of the high tragedy, even courage, of the old man.

Jody, on the other hand, has been touched by Gitano's presence, almost as if the old man had been sent precisely to him to give him some sense of the greatness of the mountains, sent as an answer to Jody's early curiosity, his hunger for some experience with mystery. Gitano somehow verifies human qualities greater than those his father displays or tolerates in others. After Gitano has gone, Jody again gazes at the mountains and simultaneously thinks of the old man.

The life of great poetic meaning, exemplified by Gitano, seems to be one with tradition and the past. Joining Gitano on his journey into the mountains, where the body will surely die, is the old horse, Easter, whose name denotes a spiritual resurrection in the future.

The "nameless sorrow" that seizes Jody at the story's conclusion may arise from his sense that the meaning Gitano finds in tradition, the resurrection of the spirit suggested by Easter, and the spiritual aspiration evoked by the Great Mountains have no place in Carl Tiflin's world.

THE RED PONY: "THE PROMISE"

"The Promise," the third story in *The Red Pony*, resembles "The Gift" in narrative structure. The theme of the story, another step in Jody's initiation into adulthood, is the intermingling of new life and death—the inevitable presence of death as part of life. The theme of initiation and growth continues in this third sequence as Jody trades in his childish war games with insects for serious work on the ranch, graduating to driving a rake and milking a cow in addition to the child's chores of feeding chickens and bringing in wood and eggs. As soon as his father promised him Nellie's colt, "his shoulders swayed a little with maturity and importance," and he "was far too grown up" to collect insects. The next day again finds him thinking of his "maturity." To Billy's assertion that Jody will have to wait two years to ride the colt, he replies, "I'll be grown up" (66).

Central to Jody's initiation is Billy Buck, Jody's idol, whom he had found wanting in the first story. At the end of "The Gift" Billy had overseen the death of the pony, finding himself responsible for the pony's death in not coming home as he had promised to get the animal out of the rain. He had also promised what he could not deliver: to keep away sickness and death—mortality—from Jody's life. Despite Billy's recent shattering awareness of his own limitations, his optimism again gets the best of him when Jody extracts a promise from him of a good colt. This time Billy keeps his promise, but at a dear price, for, again, he is unable to keep away the inevitability of death. He has a choice when he sees that the colt is turned wrong, but he knows that no matter what choice he makes, to save the colt or its mother, death will intrude.

Life and death are randomly mixed in the story, almost like a roll of the dice. Sometimes life triumphs, sometimes death. There is a cruel randomness in nature and life in general. Nature had created several normal births for the mare Nellie. Yet Jody's colt, for no apparent reason, is turned wrong, bringing on death. Jody has come to expect the presence of this randomness in his life. He will be punished sometimes for no apparent reason. On the first day of the story, however, again for no reason that he can predict, he is rewarded rather than punished.

The unavoidable juxtaposition of life and death contributes to the irony of the title, in that Billy's promise, as well as the promise of new life represented by the colt, must inevitably encompass death. For example, in the first scene, when Jody marches home from school alone, everything around him is "gold with spring." He sees the "golden green" of the oak trees, "new silver leaves," lambs, and young calves (56, 57). Yet Jody's chief action is to bring death, suffocating a toad and insects in his lunch box. In this landscape, his imagination springs to life. But the products of his imagination are deadly: "a phantom army with great flags and swords, silent but deadly" (56), and a rifle for hunting (57).

In the scene that follows, the promise of new life dominates with the prospect of a colt to call his own. As he leads Nellie to be bred the next day, the whole landscape sings with spring renewal.

But even in the mating of the horses, an act that will create the new colt, there is the potential for destruction and death. As the horses converge in violence, Mr. Taylor rescues Jody from the horses' legs by putting him on his own horse with the words, "You might have gotten killed," and Jody, concerned for Nellie, cries out, "He'll hurt her, he'll kill her" (63). Ironically, of course, the breeding does result in Nellie's death.

Nellie is wild and has the potential to kill before she is bred; afterwards she is docile and creative. With summer's fullness, shown in the ripening wild oats, Nellie herself gives evidence of new life, and Jody seeks to know more about what the birth itself will be like, asking repeatedly "how it'll be." He also repeatedly extracts from Billy the promise of "a good colt"—the promise which will lead to Nellie's death. Jody's questions, in themselves, arise from his experience with the red pony, and they remind Billy of his responsibility for the death and his inability to avert it.

Billy, in preparing Jody for the possibility that something could go wrong, sets up a situation that shows the lengths to which he will go in the end to keep his promise. He warns of the potential for gruesome death to intrude in the birth process. Usually, Billy explains, if the colt is not positioned for an easy birth, it is torn to pieces to extract it from the womb in order to save the mare.

Even though both Billy and Jody are optimistic that this birth will not be marred by death, Jody already has evidence of the pairing of renewal and death in the landscape he sees every day. These opposites are represented by the spring stream on one hand and the black cypress tree on the other. The spring whose waters are piped into the old green tub is a symbol of new life, water being an ancient symbol of renewal, as, for example, in the ritual of baptism. The "old" person goes beneath the baptismal waters, and a "new" person emerges. The spring's connection with renewal can also be seen in the patch of grass it makes green. As it renews the grass, so it brings new life to Jody.

In opposition to the life-giving force of the spring is the death-bringer—the black cypress tree where the pigs are slaughtered. Jody must go to the life-giver, the spring, as a charm to counteract the force of the death-bringer.

At the spring, his imagination, which had been fertile with the creation of tigers and lions in the first scene, now brings into being a magnificent colt named Black Demon, the name itself suggestive more of a death than a life force, even though this stallion of Jody's imagination helps him become a hero fighting for good against the forces of evil.

The coupling of life and death is suggested to Jody once more when, as he awaits the arrival of the colt under the mentorship of Billy, he learns that Billy's life began with his mother's death, a tragedy that will be reenacted when Nellie dies and her colt is born. Billy's early boast that he is half-horse himself, along with his close connection with Nellie, makes the action he later takes to keep his promise somehow more tragic, almost as if he is killing one of his own kind or causing the death of his own mother again.

The duality of existence becomes more apparent as the world's death deepens in January. Though Jody has reason to anticipate the birth of the colt, the fear of death haunts him, and he has nightmares. When he goes out into the darkness to check on Nellie, the black cypress, reminding him of death, looms over the scene. Seeing that Nellie is in pain, shivering at his touch, he becomes more apprehensive that death as well as life is in the air. As he returns to the house, haunted by memories of the red pony's death, the black cypress again dominates the landscape.

The terrible presence of death at the birth scene occurs as Billy must crush Nellie's skull and rip open her belly to retrieve the colt, going against usual practice in such cases in order to keep his promise to Jody. Both Jody and Billy are more traumatized and pained by Nellie's death than they are jubilant over the arrival of the colt. As Jody goes to fetch the life-giving water with which to baptize his colt, he can only think of death. The newborn colt, Black Demon, is the bringer of its mother's death. The further implication of the intrusion of death in the process of bringing forth new life is that the cause of Nellie's death must ultimately rest on Jody himself because he has exacted the promise from Billy.

THE RED PONY: "THE LEADER OF THE PEOPLE"

Of the four stories that comprise the shaping of the young boy Jody, the final one, "The Leader of the People," follows "The Great Mountains" in theme, just as "The Promise" follows "The Gift." The final story affirms a high human potential that gives certain people an exalted, heroic stature above nature and natural law and above the ordinary survivor's everyday practicalities. "The Leader of the People" brings the action around to spring again, one year after Jody has marched off to have Nellie bred. As in "The Great Mountains," the interaction is between Jody and an old man—this time his grandfather—who, even though he is approaching death, evinces a life of aspiration and accomplishment far greater than that of his adversarial son-in-law, Carl Tiflin. Herein lies the irony of both stories: that the higher, more vigorous life force abides in men who are old and dying.

As in the other three stories, the tree of death, the black cypress, haunts the landscape, even in spring. Innocent destructiveness is introduced as a theme when Jody plans to flail the mice out of the remains of the haystack for the dogs to kill. Parallel to this physical action is the senseless humiliation inflicted by Jody's mother and father, who diminish his spirit with ridicule and fear. He is, for no reason that the narrator gives the reader, threatened and humiliated for being a "Big-Britches." His mother responds to his good-hearted intentions by attributing selfish motives to Jody's generous gesture toward her father (100). While Jody seems to be accustomed to these spirit-killing taunts, he is not impervious to them. They make him feel embarrassed, miserable, ashamed, "collapsed and empty" (92).

As in the other stories, Carl Tiflin is placed in an adversarial position as the enemy of what he sees as impracticality and softness—aspiration, adventure, and history—in short, the finer human spirit that soars above the mundane life of everyday grubbing for existence. Carl complains of his father-in-law's endless talking about his past involvement with Indians and pioneers who settled the West. He resists the old man's efforts to keep that adventurous spirit alive.

The grandfather stands for everything Carl Tiflin hates. And the grandfather is the one who embodies greatness and the hope for passing along to subsequent generations the adventuresome spirit that led to his and his generation's courageous trek toward the West. Grandfather was the leader of these brave people, facing hostile Indians and famine on a wagon train in their quest for the unknown. Jody thinks of his grandfather and the other pioneers as heroes, "a race of giants" (94).

The tragedy is that this great pioneering way of life has died out. Something small and petty has taken its place. Even before his grandfather tells him that "westering has died out of the people" (100), Jody realizes this—that perhaps only Billy Buck has something of the necessary greatness in him.

Those in control in the present generation, unlike the pioneers, are smaller men, interested in diminishing life, killing the spirit, and belittling the importance of the tradition and the past.

The common element in the four stories that comprise *The Red Pony* is the affirmation of the human heart, great in imagination, sensitivity, aspiration, and spiritual meaning. This is real "life." It must always battle and seek to rise above an opposite death force found in devouring, dog-eat-dog nature and in the deadening smallness of men whose vision is limited to the mundane practicalities of natural survival.

OF MICE AND MEN

The same theme also dominates *Of Mice and Men*, Steinbeck's highly popular and much dramatized book of 1937. Steinbeck wrote of his work, "This is at once the sadness, the greatness, and the triumph of our species."[1] It is the story of the human potential to rise above the animal level to a finer spirit. The new element introduced in the story, however, is the power of a society, formed of nature's baser forces, to destroy this finer human spirit.

Three main topics establish the theme: (1) the animal identities and animal-like traits of the characters; (2) the dreams of rising above the animal level; and (3) the society whose animalistic drive for survival and conquest crushes the human spirit.

Lennie, large, simpleminded, and clumsy, is the character whose physical appearance is most like an animal. He is first described as looking like a bear with big paws, walking heavily. In the same scene he is also compared to a small dog—"a terrier who doesn't want to bring a ball to its master" (9). Lennie's "fawning" approach to Crooks, in the doorway of the black man's quarters, is also like that of a shy dog who desperately wants to make friends with a hostile human. And at the end of the story, when George puts the gun behind his head to kill him, Lennie is identified with Candy's old dog, who has earlier been killed in the same way with the same gun. Lennie's simplemindedness as well as his attraction to animals, especially the rabbits and the puppy, would seem to fix him as animal-like.

Candy is another character who is identified with an animal who, like Candy, is old and sick and considered useless. Candy and the reader note the similarities between him and his crippled old dog, "a dragfooted sheep dog, gray of muzzle, and with pale, blind old eyes" (24). "Got no teeth," Carlson says of the dog. "He's all stiff with rheumatism. He ain't no good to you, Candy. An' he ain't no good to himself" (44).

The irony is that Lennie and Candy, compared with a lumbering bear and a lame sheep dog, are not the truly animal-like characters in the story, for these two weak men at least exhibit human sympathy and compassion. Those who display the basest elements of nature are Curley and Carlson, who lack all sensitivity, all compassion for those more helpless and weaker in mind and body than they are. Carlson shows his animal-like nature in pushing Candy into allowing him to shoot his beloved old dog. Curley is the epitome of man's lower nature: he is driven to compete constantly, as if he lives in a world where only the physically fittest survive and, as with the lower animals, must act only for self-survival and self-gratification. Curley is like an undersized tomcat who has to challenge everyone he sees to a fight. Like a chicken, he is compelled to pick on weaklings in his own species, like Lennie, whom he discovers to be simpleminded. Like some wild animal, Curley is in a constant state of suspicion, and like all lower animals, he lives only to gratify himself, joining the single ranch hands in visiting a house of prostitution in the nearest town even though he is recently married. And like an ill-tempered and scared wild animal, Curley is "mean"—a word used repeatedly to describe him. Animal-like, Carlson and Curley seem incapable of sensitivity, of empathizing with another human being. The last words in the novel belong to Carlson, who has just seen a man devastated by having to kill his friend. Watching George walk away with Slim, Carlson says, "Now what the hell ya suppose is eatin' them two guys?" (107).

Candy, Curley's wife, and, for a brief moment, Crooks all reveal a need to dream, which in this novel symbolizes reaching for something above brute nature. But it is George and Lennie who best embody the finer spirit that aspires and sustains human connections. It has been said that Lennie's obsession with mice and rabbits represents his yearning for human warmth.[2] Of all the characters in the novel, only George and Lennie have a human bond that could be classified as being in the spirit of a family. They alone travel together, share a history, have responsibility and commitment to each other, and need each other. In the first scene before they reach the ranch, George and Lennie reassure each other of their situation: "We got somebody to talk to that gives a damn about us . . . because I got you to look after me, and you got me to look after you" (14). Candy, the old swamper, hopes to become part of their family. Their rise above animal nature is consistent with their rise above ego, soaring above mere self to concern for someone else.

More than this, George and Lennie show that they reach above the brute animal level in their aspiration for something better than lonely self-gratification and survival from one day to the next. They look forward to owning a little piece of land with a house on it and providing for their own needs. "There wouldn't be no more runnin' round the country" (57), and "We'd know what come of our planting" (58), George says.

Establishing a human family in a stable house on one's own land suggests as well the ability to make one's own decisions and choices, independence, and maturity. No longer would they lead the shifting life of children, always being ordered around by someone else, depending on a boss to make decisions and tell them what they must do, and being dependent on someone else for the means to make a living.

Even though George and Lennie have gone farther in clinging to their aspirations for a better life in which they would make their own decisions, others also have dreams, as evidenced by the men who read romantic stories in the western magazines and Crooks' comments on the hundreds of men he has seen over the years who have tried and failed to settle down on their own piece of land: "Ever'body wants a little piece of lan'. . . . Nobody never gets to heaven, and nobody gets no land. It's just in their head" (74).

If the ranch in the valley represents nature—hard physical labor just for basic survival—the Gabilan Mountains that surround it represent the human aspiration for something better.

At the same time that Lennie and George (and for a brief time Candy and Crooks) aspire to escape the life that most men in their situation are doomed to, there are foreshadowings at every turn to predict their defeat: Lennie's trouble with a girl in Weed; his unintentional killing of mice, then of the puppy; Curley's taunting of him and George's warning that Lennie might do damage if Curley continues; and the provocativeness of Curley's wife and Lennie's fascination with her.

This is a society that reduces men and women to the lowest level by squelching aspirations and discouraging human connections and sympathy. One of the ironies of the valley is that here a person is called "mature" and "realistic" when he continues life as a boy, gives up his dreams of independence, acts harshly rather than sympathetically, especially toward the weak, and continues to substitute self-gratification for commitment. So this society, represented by the machine, cripples its members—Candy literally and the other men metaphorically—in that in taking away their opportunities for independence and human connections, it is taking away their manhood.

Their lack of independence is shown in the fact that, though they can move from job to job, they must always follow the schedule of the boss. They own nothing except what they can carry on their backs. They drift from place to place with, as George says, no future and no place to go. The farm boss feeds them and gives them a place to sleep, like young boys in an orphanage dormitory. There is little in the way of independent decision making, as there would be for George and Lennie if they owned their own place and could, as George says, just take off and go to a show if one came to town.

Like boys, none of them has a stable home with wife and children. They spend their nights off in self-gratification in barrooms and houses of prostitution, most of them free from commitment to any man or woman. By contrast, George thinks of the boyish freedom he could return to if he didn't have Lennie to worry about. Most of the hands have no one to care about and no one to care about them.

This kind of life has two results. One is that it brings out the worst, the lowest, and the most self-centered aspects of human nature. This kind of life kills off kindness, creating monsters like Carlson, who shoots Candy's old dog. Another result of the failure of commitment and connection is loneliness, a word used by George, Crooks, and Slim. The men aren't the only lonely ones; loneliness is the downfall of Curley's wife. Significantly, Soledad, the name of the closest town, means "solitary" in Spanish. Solitude also seems indicative of their lives in that, even though they live together in one room, the only card game they play all the way to the end in the bunkhouse is solitaire.

The title *Of Mice and Men* comes from "To a Mouse," a poem by the eighteenth-century Scottish poet Robert Burns. Burns writes, after unintentionally ploughing up the nest of a mouse, that "the best-laid schemes o' mice an' men / Gang aft a-gley" (or go awry), "An' lea'e us nought" (and leave us nothing) "but grief an' pain, / For promised joy." The title of Steinbeck's novella, then, not only is a reference to the poor mice that Lennie accidentally kills, but to everyone whose dreams are vanquished and who is left with only grief and pain.

Readers of *Of Mice and Men* have argued about whether the ending is bleak and fatalistic (that is, that George will now just become like all the rest of the lonely "boys" and grow old, poor, and dispensable like Candy and Crooks) or whether it is hopeful (that George and Slim will now forge a friendship that will allow them to aspire to a better life). Regardless of how one interprets the conclusion, which Steinbeck leaves mysterious and unspoken, the story, like those in *The Red Pony*, is an affirmation of the qualities of "our species" to rise above base nature.

THE PEARL

Like the 1937 *Of Mice and Men*, *The Pearl*, published ten years later, is a story of what distinguishes the human species from all others. It is a story, set in Mexico, of a poor man's aspiration, his dreams of being "a man" instead of a child, and his dream of escaping a 400-year-old cycle of poverty—rags, illness, hunger, and especially ignorance. It is yet another story of "the sadness, the greatness, and the triumph of our species." But it is also a tale of the destructive impediments that a powerful and greedy society relentlessly throws up to thwart all such efforts on the part of the poor and downtrodden.

Kino, the peasant who finds "the Pearl of the World," is a man who from first to last values his family above all other things, for "the Song of the Family" is always playing in his head from first to last, even when destructive forces around him attempt to drown it out. What changes when he finds the pearl and differentiates him from his neighbors is that he is no longer content with poverty and, most of all, refuses to accept the same lifelong poverty for his child. As the story opens, before he finds the pearl, the reader has some sense of the family's poverty: they live in a house made of brush with a dirt floor, segregated from those of European descent, who live in some measure of comfort in town. Kino's breakfast, in contrast to the doctor's lavish meal, is a corncake. His wife wears a faded skirt and a ragged shawl, and his own clothes betray their age and many washings.

In further elaborating on the conditions in which Kino and his neighbors live, the narrator makes plain that his own retelling of a Mexican folktale has a social edge to it. The exploitation of Kino and his neighbors has gone on for centuries. The European doctor from whom they unsuccessfully seek help is described as being like others of his powerful class, who "for nearly four hundred years had beaten and starved and robbed and despised Kino's race, and frightened it too" (9). The waters in which Kino dives for pearls were once exploited by the king of Spain—these pearls "had helped to pay for his wars, and had decorated the churches for his soul's sake" (16). When the doctor, hearing of Kino's pearl, finally visits the house on the pretense of healing the baby, Kino's eyes flame with hatred for the "hundreds of years of subjugation" (30) by strangers who had come from Europe "with argument and authority and gunpowder to back up both" (46).

And the exploitation of the poor has continued over the years in recent history and Kino's memory. One pearl merchant owns all the petty buyers in the village, who have a policy of deciding together in secret what price they will give the peasants for pearls and of keeping the price as low as possible. When the poor divers tried to better their lot by having one of their number take their pearls to the city to sell, the emissary disappeared on his first trip, and the second emissary disappeared as well. "And so they gave the whole thing up and went back to the old way" (46). Not only did the powerful and rich merchants object to the peasants' attempts to better themselves in this way, but the merchants were supported by the priest in the village. When the buyers get together to deny Kino a fair price for his pearl, the villagers suspect that "we have been cheated all our lives" (53).

In Kino's own village, the poor have been denied the sacraments of marriage and infant baptism because they haven't the money to pay the church for them. And the church and the priest have reinforced the power of those of European descent and joined in the oppression. The poor are not regarded as adult men and women by the priest—he treats them like children—and the wealthy people the priest supports regard Kino's race as even lower—"simple animals" (9).

The message that the priest, representing the church, uses to keep the poor down is well known to the peasants. He tells them that God has put them in a particular place in this world—as peasants—and that God wants them to remain there. To try to better themselves, for example, by taking their pearls to the capital to sell, is to rebel against God, who intends for them to stay poor.

These powerful forces keep the peasants in continual poverty by keeping them in ignorance. None of the poor people know how to read or write, so, as Kino believes, none of them know if what they are always told (by those who want to keep them in poverty) is true. Now he doesn't know what things are actually in the book and what things are not (27). He believes that illiteracy keeps his people in a trap. Kino believes that he can't be sure whether what the doctor, the priest, and the buyers tell him is "the truth of things" (37). Kino is acutely aware of this on the day he finds the pearl, when the doctor visits his house and insists that the baby needs to be treated to keep it from developing further effects of the scorpion bite. He suspects that the doctor is cheating them, but he doesn't really know, and he might be taking a chance with his son's life in rejecting the doctor's offer.

Likewise, when he prepares to take the pearl to the buyers (whom the divers all suspect to be dishonest), Kino's brother says,

"*We do not know* what prices are paid in other places. . . . *How can we know* what is a fair price. . . .*" And Kino replies, "[B]ut *how can we know?*" (45; emphasis added).

The trap of ignorance is personified by the mysterious dealer in pearls who, though he controls their lives, is completely unknown to them. Unknown adversaries are also personified by evil figures who attack Kino after he finds the pearl. The first figure who comes into the house is described as being disembodied—a foot and fingers. When the figure runs away, Kino says, "The thing has gone" (38). When he is attacked the second time outside his house, he tells Juana, "I don't know. . . . I didn't see" (56). He does not know his attackers in the third instance on the path either, identifying them merely as "a dark figure," "frantic figures," "greedy fingers" (59). The ones who follow the family out of town are equally unknown and mysterious. He calls them "the trackers" and "the dark ones" (63). In sum, he and his neighbors never really know who ultimately controls their lives; they never know who attacks them or who the enemy is. Kino only hears some evil song, senses some destructive forces at work, not unlike the scorpion.

Though Kino certainly knows all this, on the morning before his child is bitten by the scorpion he seems absolutely contented, as does his wife, Juana, who sings an ancient song of "safety," "warmth," and wholeness (3).

The community's resignation to poverty is shown in these songs, which, like others in the community, are ancient ones. But, Kino notes, there are "no new songs." Yet from this day forward, Kino does hear a new song, and the way Kino looks at life changes drastically. The first step in that change is not the finding of the pearl, but what occurs as a result of a scorpion biting his baby, Coyotito, for they are turned away from the doctor's house because they have no money. At that moment, Kino's action is contrary to the acquiescent lives of the people in his community. In a gesture of rebellion that foreshadows his subsequent independence and outrage at those who hold power, he strikes the gate with his fist. He splits his knuckles in doing this, and they bleed, an augury of the pain his rebellion will cause him. Throughout the rest of the day, he will notice his split knuckles and be faintly reminded of his rebellious action.

So, Kino's rebellious ascendency to human greatness can be traced, finally, not to the Song of the Pearl but to the Song of the

Family, not to his finding of the pearl, but to his earlier fear for his child. It is the child's illness and the doctor's refusal to treat him that then leads to Kino's intense search and Juana's fervent prayers to find a valuable pearl. And it is primarily his ambition that his son not live his life in ignorance that leads Kino to insist on using the pearl he finds to better his family's life.

Juana is afraid and would sacrifice the pearl and any significant betterment in their lives in order to keep alive the song of safety, warmth, wholeness, caution, reason, and preservation. But Kino's initial act of rebellion after his rejection by the doctor, in combination with the pearl, leads to his moment of greatness, brief as it is. In that moment he becomes a man, shaking off the forces that regard him as a child or an animal to be kept in his place. After he has three times defeated the faceless forces who have attacked him in the dark, after he has made up his mind to defy them in order to get a just price for the pearl for his family, he is able to call himself a man; he repeats three times in succession, "I am a man" (57).

What makes Kino's relatives fear for him is that he is not just defying a group of pearl buyers or fighting thugs who attack him in the dark; he is challenging the whole system of exploitation. As his brother Juan Tomás explains to him, they are all cheated from the time they are born.

Kino's human greatness emerges in that, for a time, he tries to take control of his own destiny and make decisions on his own, which, in effect, gives him a godlike quality. His plans are dreams of breaking out of his poverty—to give his family what he could never afford. First, he would be able to marry Juana and to have his son baptized in the church. Then he would provide them with the essential needs of every human being: a "guarantee of the future, of comfort, of security. . . . [A] poultice against illness and a wall against insult." The pearl would allow him to close "a door on hunger" (39). But above all other things, his son "must go to school. He must break out of the pot that holds us in" (39). By this means, Coyotito would be able to tell Kino what the book really says. Kino's aspirations ennoble him; it is this self-awareness and desire for a better life that distinguishes man and separates him from the lower animals.

As the scorpion's attack on the child and the doctor's refusal to treat him had precipitated the action, so the child's death at the hand of human scorpions ends the action, including Kino's plans and his defiance. His actions have not necessarily made him a good man or a kinder man (as his vicious blow to Juana's face reveals). Nor, in the end, has he been triumphant. But momentarily Kino has been a man. At least for a moment, he has done what few people ever do at all—he has achieved greatness.

For all their differences in settings, characters, and tone, these three novellas are alike in affirming the ability of humans to be more than animals.

NOTES

1. John Steinbeck, *Steinbeck: A Life in Letters*, edited by Elaine Steinbeck (New York: Viking, 1975), 562–563.

2. Louis Owens, *John Steinbeck's Re-vision of America* (Athens: University of Georgia Press, 1985).

TOPICS FOR WRITTEN OR ORAL EXPLORATION

1. Write an essay comparing and contrasting Billy Buck with Carl Tiflin.

2. Some critics claim that Carl Tiflin is the man to admire in *The Red Pony*. If there is sufficient difference of opinion in class, debate this issue.

3. How, in your opinion, do individuals romanticize animals or nature unrealistically?

4. Write an essay on Steinbeck's portrayal of old people in *The Red Pony* and *Of Mice and Men*. What do the portraits have in common? Are they generally sympathetically drawn? Explain.

5. Stage a dramatic reading of one of the four stories in *The Red Pony*, using the dialogue alone.

6. Design sets for a hypothetical stage production of *The Red Pony*. Be prepared to justify your choices.

7. Secure a copy of the play of *Of Mice and Men*. What changes were made in the book to dramatize it? Do the changes alter the meaning of the play in your estimation? Explain.

8. Write your own play script of *Of Mice and Men* and stage a class production of it.

9. What is unknown about George and Lennie's past? What effect do these mysteries have on their story?

10. What do you presume to be their history? Why?

11. What is your interpretation of what happens to George after the completion of the story? Support your assumptions with evidence from the text.

12. Do you read *Of Mice and Men* as a pessimistic or an optimistic story? Why or why not?

13. In *Of Mice and Men*, Slim agrees with George that the simpleminded Lennie is a nice fellow and further claims that smart people are often less nice than others. Is there any truth to his assessment? Explain your answer, giving examples.

14. Write an essay on what Lennie contributes to George's life.

15. Read Steinbeck's account in *The Sea of Cortez* of the Mexican legend on which he based *The Pearl*. How has he changed the legend? How do the changes alter an interpretation of Kino?

16. Why exactly does illiteracy usually keep a person or a people powerless? Can you give any specific examples?

17. How does the peculiar knowledge of doctors, priests, or lawyers give them a special kind of power? Again, cite examples.

18. The tragic hero is often defined as a basically good person who struggles against powerful entities (including fate), knowing that he will probably lose. Are any of the characters in Steinbeck's short novels such heroes? Why or why not?

19. Write an essay on Steinbeck's portrayal of women in the three novellas.

20. When Steinbeck wrote *Of Mice and Men* and *The Pearl*, he had in mind eventual dramatizations of these pieces. Examine the dramatic structure of each one—the use of scenes, stage directions, units of dialogue, initiating circumstances, and rising action.

21. Each of the three novellas involves literal families or substitute family units. Compare and contrast the "families" in all three.

22. Write an essay on the community as a "character" in *The Pearl*.

23. Would it have been better if Kino had never found the pearl? If there is sufficient difference of opinion on this issue, have a debate on the subject.

SUGGESTIONS FOR FURTHER READING

Benson, Jackson J. *Looking for Steinbeck's Ghost*. Norman: University of Oklahoma Press, 1988.

Fontenrose, Joseph Eddy. *John Steinbeck: An Introduction and Interpretation*. New York: Barnes and Noble, 1963.

French, Warren G. *John Steinbeck*. New York: Twayne, 1961.

Hughes, R. S. *Beyond "The Red Pony."* Metuchen, N. J.: Scarecrow Press, 1987.

———. *John Steinbeck: A Study of the Short Fiction*. Boston: Twayne, 1989.

Jaina, Sunita. *John Steinbeck's Concept of Man: A Critical Study of His Novels*. New Delhi: New Statesman, 1979.

McCarthy, Paul. *John Steinbeck*. New York: F. Ungar, 1980.

Marks, Lester Jay. *Thematic Design in the Novels of John Steinbeck*. The Hague: Mouton, 1969.

Owens, Louis. *John Steinbeck's Re-vision of America*. Athens: University of Georgia Press, 1985.

Parini, Jay. *John Steinbeck: A Biography*. New York: H. Holt, 1995.

Prabhakar, S. S. *John Steinbeck: A Study*. Hyderabad: Academic, 1976.

St. Pierre, Brian. *John Steinbeck: The California Years*. San Francisco: Chronicle Books, 1983.

Simmonds, Roy S. *Steinbeck's Literary Achievement*. Muncie, Ind.: Ball State University Press, 1976.

Timmerman, John H. *John Steinbeck's Fiction: The Aesthetics of the Road Taken*. Norman: University of Oklahoma Press, 1986.

2

Old California and the West

John Steinbeck's work is thoroughly enmeshed in the California landscape and California culture where *The Red Pony* and *Of Mice and Men* take place. His most direct allusion to the westward movement of America occurs in *The Red Pony* in the section entitled "The Leader of the People," during a visit from Jody's grandfather. This old man once led a wagon train west to California, seemingly in 1887, and entered the state just east of Tahoe on a trail used by numerous earlier pioneering parties. In the course of the trip he underwent many trials like those frequently recorded by actual pioneers—hunger so intense that the party often ate the cattle that were pulling the wagons, thievery by Indians, and drought. The old man speaks constantly of his westward adventure, bemoaning the end of the frontier, therefore the end of heroic aspiration. Jody, in his innocence, recognizes that those who risked so much to come to largely uncharted land out west were giants and heroes of immense vitality who, with the demise of the frontier, are gone. As the old man explains, what was important wasn't the Indians, it was the enormous *life* in the people at the time. What was important, he says, was movement, westering.

While "The Leader of the People" is the most specific allusion to pioneering, both *The Red Pony* and *Of Mice and Men* emerge from a newly developed western culture that has left European

California was regarded as a paradise in the late nineteenth century. This drawing was entitled "A Dream of the Tropics."

traditions and East Coast stability far behind. The nineteenth-century urge to move ever farther west in search of a new life, land, and gold culminated in Steinbeck's native California, where it came to an end at the edge of the Pacific Ocean.

THE NATURE OF THE WEST AND THE CALIFORNIA NOVELLAS

Those aspects of Steinbeck's work which derive from the west-ering movement include the following: (1) the religious meaning in the western frontier; (2) mobility (wandering and rootlessness); (3) the escape from a personal history; (4) the prevalence of risk-taking, danger, and violence; (5) the pursuit of another Garden of Eden that involves the independence that comes with land own-ership. Both novellas are also strongly influenced by the demise of the frontier and the frontier spirit.

The religious meaning of unexplored frontier largely untouched by civilized man is especially pertinent to both the early pioneers and to two stories in *The Red Pony*. The grandfather, the old pai-sano, and Jody as well sense something spiritual in the mountains rarely touched by man. In that sense the mountains themselves are still an untouched, almost holy frontier. The grandfather explains that the pioneers who made the crossing with him wept when they saw the mountains. It was, in a sense, a religious experience for them. Similarly, in the story entitled "The Great Mountains," Jody is obsessed with the mountains as representative of the unknow-able, godlike frontier. And the old paisano approaches the moun-tain frontier as a holy place where he goes to die.

The violence associated with the frontier and the danger and risks involved in living close to nature are everywhere apparent in these two stories of California. Danger is always close when work-ing with horses. Risks are always involved when working with farm machinery. Human violence, epitomized in the nineteenth century by the gun fighter and rustler, is seen in *Of Mice and Men* in Curley's attack on Lennie, Lennie's killing of Curley's wife, and the lynching party that proceeds to hunt for Lennie.

Dreams of land and gold, climate and adventure, and opportu-nities for farming and business lured pioneers to California, and the same unlikely dreams tempt the men in *Of Mice and Men*. Crooks says that all the men dream of owning a little land. For

George and Lennie it has become an obsession. Steinbeck also broaches the idea of California as a perceived Eden with peaceful scenes of the young Jody on the ranch and the initial description of George and Lennie sitting by the quiet pool.

Finally, both California novellas show the effect of the decline of a frontier that once gave meaning to people's lives. The grandfather in "The Leader of the People" has felt frustrated ever since he approached the Pacific Ocean and knew that there were no further western lands to explore, and he is saddened that the adventuresome spirit of the trailblazers has died out of people younger than himself. The great mountains represent the frontier—the beckoning, unexplored region which Jody wants to know more about and where the old paisano goes to die. In *Of Mice and Men* the end of the frontier has left those who remain without true self-determination and without a reasonable expectation of land or a better life.

A NEW EDEN

It might be argued that the American impulse to move west to the frontier began with those English and European settlers who immigrated across the Atlantic Ocean to the shores of Florida, Virginia, and New England in the seventeenth century. That impulse never died, for pioneers immediately pushed west, at first merely inland to the Piedmont, just short of the Appalachian Mountains, and by the 1840s all the way to the western edge of the continent.

What compelled people to move west? What attraction did the frontier hold? Part of the impulse was economic: available land above all, there for the taking west of older, more established settlements. There were stories that wealth lay in that direction—furs, timber, and precious metals, especially gold. Sometimes the West beckoned as a way to escape unpleasant realities in known civilization. Out on the frontier one could escape debts, oppression, scandal, relationships gone sour, burdensome responsibilities, and arrest. A popular folk song in California in the 1840s is revealing of a frequent motive for moving west:

Oh, what was your name in the States?
Was it Thompson or Johnson or Bates?

Did you murder your wife and fly for your life?
Say, what was your name in the States?

From the eighteenth-century beginnings of the great westward movement, dual, contradictory urges characterized the pioneers. On one hand, they had an insatiable hunger for land ownership, which could bring with it stability, wealth, and respectability. In the Old World there was little or no possibility for a poor person to own land, but America, and in particular the frontier to the west of civilized cities, held out the promise of land ownership and all that went with it to the sons and daughters of Europe's poor. Land was the way to independence. Crops for food, cotton and wool for cloth, animals for meat and hides, wood for building one's own shelter—all could be produced on land in the New World. A farmer with his own land did not have to depend on someone else for his subsistence. He was his own boss, owned himself, and was free to create his own destiny.

On the other hand, the pioneers' hunger for adventure led them to desert the land and the stability they had acquired to risk going further into the unknown. The frontier stretched one's possibilities and imagination, for just beyond the tree line, so to speak, lay opportunities to unravel mysteries and to garner wealth.

Even before the American Revolution began, speculators were sending scouts into unexplored territories in the West to seek out the possibilities for a lucrative fur trade and to speculate in land. Daniel Boone, the famous trailblazer, began his career as a scout for just such a speculator, Richard Henderson. Their efforts were part of the first major westward movement, beginning in 1775, which opened the way to settlement of Kentucky and Tennessee. By 1783 pioneers had made their way to the Mississippi River and had established major settlements in what are now Nashville, Tennessee, and Louisville, Kentucky.

The key element was always land. Land ownership, the aim of both individual families and speculators, continued to be the incentive for westering. And controversies over land formed the major conflicts of the period: struggles between Native Americans and encroaching settlers, between settlers and land speculators, between farmers and hunters, and between speculators and state governments. Land was also at the center of a major legislative controversy about just how the western plots were to be divided and whether settlers were to be charged for their uncharted claims.

Soon after American independence was achieved, land west of the Appalachians began to be densely settled. In only two months in the summer of 1795, an estimated twenty-six hundred settlers moved into Tennessee. Throughout the year tens of thousands moved into the Ohio Valley by river. By 1802 trading posts had been established in what are now Mobile, Alabama, Memphis, Tennessee, Fort Wayne, Indiana, and Detroit, Michigan.

In 1803 peculiar events put in motion another wave of western expansion beyond the Mississippi River into land held first by the Spaniards and then by the French. Thomas Jefferson had already proposed a major expedition into the area when Napoleon approached United States envoys with an offer to sell 909,000 square miles in the New World. In 1804, shortly after the United States bought the Louisiana territory for $15 million, two explorers, Meriwether Lewis and William Clark, started up the Missouri River with a small party of men. (They would eventually take on one Indian woman as a guide.) They reached what are now Montana and Wyoming and in 1805 reached the shores of the Pacific Ocean.

Still, the Louisiana Purchase did not immediately attract the great number of western farmers that the opening of the Appalachian Mountains had, for much of the land was inaccesible or barren or contained soil to which eastern farmers were not accustomed. Three areas of the Purchase did attract settlers, however. One was the strip along the Gulf of Mexico encompassing Florida, coastal Alabama, Louisiana, and Texas, all of which seemed suitable for cotton growing. Another was the northern area between Lakes Huron and Erie with their port cities on the lakes. Finally, there was the Indian territory remaining east of the Mississippi River which included Alabama and Mississippi.

Spurred largely by unemployment in the East, another wave westward occurred after the War of 1812. In the years between 1810 and 1820 the number of settlers west of the Appalachian Mountains increased by over a million.

While whole families moved west to farm, the scouts and explorers that preceded them, and the mountain men, soldiers, fur traders, and trappers constituted large categories of men traveling alone or with groups of other men, all of whom were constantly on the move and constantly in danger.

The ultimate western place, the end of the line for western travelers, was California. From the time of the earliest explorers to the twentieth century, in, for example, a song by Woody Guthrie, California was described as "a Garden of Eden." This image may have been suggested in part by the exotic crops that flourished there—wine grapes, apricots, olives, and almonds, for example—and the exotic birds and flowers found there. The image of the state as an Eden or paradise is underscored by the perpetual use of the word "gold." From medieval times, gold, the perfect metal, was the symbol of Eden, perfection, purity. The Golden Age, for example, refers to the mythical era of classical times when gods were supposed to have walked the earth. Explorers of California in those early times frequently sent back stories to the East of a golden garden, a paradise. One reason for its identification with gold from the start may have been the golden sunshine, especially in the southern part of the region. In any case, California came to be known as the Golden State; San Francisco's famous bridge was named the Golden Gate Bridge. The state's most prominent and exotic crop, the orange, was called the Golden Fruit. Then, of course, there was the identification of California with actual gold ore with the discovery of rich veins of the precious metal in 1848. Promoters, in attempting to attract settlers later in the nineteenth century, would talk of its golden valleys and describe it as a domestic Eden.

EARLY DAYS OF CALIFORNIA SETTLEMENT

The first Americans from the Midwest and East who entered California overland in the 1820s were those loners called scouts, mountain men, and fur traders. A rich culture was already flourishing there comprised primarily of Spanish churchmen—friars—and Native Americans. These settlers lived in an intricate network of religious missions, the life of which was supported by large herds of cattle, orchards, wineries, and other enterprises. But by 1833 the missions had lost their religious purpose. And in the place of the old churchmen and their Native American servants came ranchers, hunters, and fur traders.

To those hungry for adventure and new places for enterprise, California was indeed a paradise. Two of the most adventuresome businessmen to enter the territory in the late 1830s were John Marsh and John Sutter. In the middle of their careers as adventurers, these two men, who had known each other earlier, ended up in California, where they replaced the system of twenty-one coastal missions with commercial settlements in the fertile inland valleys. Marsh, after a brief stay in the little town of Los Angeles, settled on a range of hills near what is now Berkeley, across the bay from San Francisco. Sutter set up his businesses on a huge grant of land in wild country near what is now Sacramento. Sutter received the largest land grant in California, 49,000 acres. His elaborate, self-sufficient principality became headquarters for all Americans (among them John C. Fremont) who passed into California.

Word began to go out from explorers that pioneers could find here a land free of the snow and ice that dogged the Midwest and Northeast and of the malaria that cursed many warmer, wetter climates in the East. Those who came to California would find, they were told, vast open areas, all ready for cultivation and easy travel, and networks of waterways. Like much of the West, it also had philosophical attractions in that it was a place without boundaries.

The first large expedition to California—some fifty-four men and five women—set out from Kansas in 1841. Subsequent groups ordinarily departed from two or three towns in Missouri and Kansas, each group hiring its own mountain man as scout and guide. With a wide variety of livestock, furniture, farm equipment, and staples, they moved west on farm wagons covered with canvas. In the early days of the trip a captain was elected to lead the way. Journeys usually began early each morning with the guide and scouts riding ahead to determine the best route; the wagons usually proceeded in two parallel columns to make circling easier in case of attack. Since there was no wood, fires were made of buffalo dung. At forts along the way repairs were made, laundry done, and supplies replenished. Frequently they made stops at either John Marsh's or John Sutter's spread once in California.

It was scarcely an idyllic romp, however. Perhaps because of the fierce independence and rivalry among the young men who made up most of those traveling by wagon train, fights, challenges, and quarrels were rampant. Very rarely did a captain chosen in the early days of the journey remain captain to the end. And because of the great length of the journey from Missouri to California and the necessity to travel so many miles a day, those who had to stop on the way because of illness, injury, or equipment breakdowns were just left behind. Lives were lost to disease, to accidental and deliberate gunshot wounds, and to falls from wagons. Furniture and equipment often had to be relinquished when oxen became too frail to pull heavy loads. Those on the 1841 expedition, for example, had to abandon their wagons altogether before reaching their destination. They also had to kill and eat their mules.

MAPPING THE UNKNOWN

The first wave of mass migration to California came between 1841 and 1846, yet even at the end of this period, the area was largely unknown and unmapped. Some of the first important mapping was done by a team of scientists, soldiers, and trappers led by John Charles Fremont in 1845. Having made several earlier excursions into the area, where he stayed occasionally on Sutter's spread near Sacramento, Fremont and his group struck out farther west, supposedly to provide Congress with maps and other information in anticipation of trouble with Mexico over California and Texas.

CALIFORNIA AND THE WAR WITH MEXICO

From 1846 to 1848 California comprised part of the battlefield in the war between the United States and Mexico. In the Salinas Valley near Monterey, Fremont and his party of some sixty soldiers and mountain men encountered trouble from the resident Mexican officials. He took refuge in the Gabilan Mountains, eventually retreating farther east when the Mexicans refused to back down. But a month later, after the United States government had invited Californios to break ties with Mexico and annex themselves to the United States, Fremont returned to California to continue surveying and dabbling in the emerging military politics of the area. In January 1848 the United States forces virtually secured control of California. In February of that year, Mexico signed a treaty ceding California to the United States. California was admitted to statehood in 1850, and further western lands were acquired from Mexico in 1853 with the Gadsden Purchase.

THE DISCOVERY OF GOLD

The demand for soldiers in the war with Mexico had drained Sutter's fort of manpower. In addition, the forfeiture of debts owed

Sutter, especially on the part of Russian trappers, had left him in deep financial trouble. He sought to regain his economic position by adding further stores and buildings to his spread. This could only be accomplished by going forty miles east to a wooded area to cut trees and mill logs to be sent down the American River to the fort. His chief carpenter, James Marshall, was delegated to head the work team. The problem of inadequate manpower was solved when a battalion of Mormons who had abandoned plans for a settlement in California arrived at Sutter's place at about the time Marshall and Sutter were finalizing plans for the mill. These men comprised Marshall's crew.

On January 24, 1848, in the process of rerouting water to carry the milled logs downstream, Marshall discovered a gold nugget. Further investigation turned up more gold. Marshall and Sutter planned to keep the discovery secret. But on May 12, Sam Brannon, one of the Mormon leaders who had set up his own store in Fort Sutter, decided that information about the discovery of gold would bring him much-needed business from outsiders. Secretly he left for San Francisco, taking with him a vial of gold dust. Just a few weeks after Brannon had advertised the amazing discovery on Sutter's property, men from all parts of the Northwest, Mexico, and South America began flocking to Coloma, California. Soon they came by boat and overland. In 1849 alone 100,000 people moved west to California.

Although only a small percentage of the many who came made a fortune by mining gold, the presence of the precious metal was a decided reality. Miners unearthed incredible finds: a 28-pound lump of gold at one site, nuggets of 20 pounds each at another, 273 pounds of nuggets in seven weeks at a third. In 1852 $81 million worth of gold was mined in California.

Those who also reaped gold in California were the merchants and other businessmen who charged outrageous prices for food, supplies, and services. The rush of miners to the gold fields made prices on all goods soar. Eggs in some places sold for three dollars apiece, for instance.

For many other reasons—the intense competition, the high stakes, and the complete lack of any system of order or law enforcement—California in the nineteenth century was as violent as any part of the notoriously violent West. After the first year of the gold rush, mining camps were plagued with crime and the only justice was extralegal. When a man (and in one documented case a woman) was regarded as being a thief or a murderer, he was hanged by the community without trial. Another crime-ridden location was San Francisco, the nearest port to the mines, where sailors and miners came and went by sea; businesses exploiting both, including brothels and saloons, sprang up suddenly. In addition to thievery, rape, and murder, arson was a constant danger. After one such rampage in San Francisco, vigilantes arrested close to 100 people. In 1851 there were 44 murders in Los Angeles and not one single conviction. At times the self-appointed vigilantes themselves proved to be the worst criminals of all.

A variety of lucrative enterprises sprang up after the Civil War with the advent of the transcontinental railroad (the completion of which was marked with a golden spike): continued mining and land speculation, banking, shipping, lumbering, ranching, farming, oil drilling, and even entertainment. Between 1870 and 1890 a major land boom occurred in the state. Floods of people poured into California hoping for a golden life or at least a better life. Many who had lived in hell in other parts of the country were looking for paradise in California. These included unemployed cowboys and fruit pickers, midwestern farmers who had lost their land, and artisans who were unappreciated and unaccepted in the East. A ballad popular at the time illustrates a widespread feeling:

> Since times are so hard, I'll tell you, sweetheart,
> I've a mind to leave off my plow and my cart
> And away to California my journey I'll go
> For to better my fortune as other folks do.[1]

Another rush to California occurred in the first three decades of the twentieth century, taking the state's history up to the time in which John Steinbeck's novels are set. During this period the population swelled from 1 million to 5 million. Again there was the promise of a better life that did not always materialize. The attractions were the climate, the easy living, its natural beauty, opportunities for land and good farming, rich natural resources including water, social mobility, and the opportunity (claimed by various Chambers of Commerce) to move rapidly into good jobs.

The documents that follow are firsthand accounts and early histories of the old days in California and the West. The portraits they draw are consistent with characteristics that emerge from Steinbeck's modern portrayals of the state. The first two documents express the authors' ideas on the religious nature of the land, among them that God dwells in nature and that being close to the land brings one closer to God.

The final three documents paint California as a second Eden, a land of rich opportunities. These include accounts by writer Washington Irving, who describes Captain Bonneville's exploration of California in 1833; John Bidwell, who in 1841 made one of the first overland passages to the state; and the Reverend John Todd, who expresses the religious meaning of the frontier but whose writing seems intended to attract further settlement in California as a way of strengthening the nation.

They present the promise of a better life in California, an existence in a new Eden with the security and fulfillment to be found through ample and rich resources, whether they be land or gold.

HECTOR ST. JOHN DE CREVECOEUR AND THE
RELIGIOUS MEANING OF LAND

The afternoon was green and gold with spring. . . . The sage-
brushes shone with new silver leaves and the oaks wore hoods
of golden green.

The Red Pony, 56

Crevecoeur was born in France in 1735 and immigrated to America
in 1765. Shortly after the American Revolution he became French
Consul in New York. In the first excerpt Crevecoeur, a farmer himself, describes the religious experience available to those who live
close to the land. Crevecoeur's description of his own land along
the Hudson River is a reminder of the teeming life on the Tiflin
farm in *The Red Pony*. Here, as in California, there is abundant life
in the changing seasons and the animals, in the first appearance
of spring and in the golden colors of dawn. Nature itself, he writes,
is the temple of God. And contemplation of nature brings one to
the "Master of Nature" who blesses mankind with "light and life."

HECTOR ST. JOHN DE CREVECOEUR, *SKETCHES OF*
EIGHTEENTH-CENTURY AMERICA (1912)

Have you never felt at the returning of spring a glow of general pleasure, an indiscernible something that pervades our whole frame, an in-
ward involuntary admiration of everything which surrounds us? 'Tis then
the beauties of Nature, everywhere spread, seem to swell every sentiment
as she swells every juice. She dissolves herself in universal love and seems
to lead us to the same sentiments. Did you ever unmoved pass by a large
orchard in full bloom without feeling an uncommon ravishment, not only
arising from the exquisite perfumes surrounding you on all sides, but
from the very splendour of the scene? Who can at this time of the year
observe the ushering in of buds, the unfolding of leaves, the appearance
of flowers, the whole progress of vegetation, and remain insensible?

Have not the regular arrival and departure of certain birds ever set you
a-thinking whence they came? Have you never reflected on the sublimity
of the knowledge they possess, in order to overcome so many difficulties,
to steer so invariable a course to other more favourable regions unseen
by men, either in their flight or return? . . . Have you never worshipped

the Master of Nature in the most august of all temples, in that extensive one of His own framing where He no doubt presides as the great invisible Pontiff, but where He permits His awful representative to become visible in order to bless mankind with light and life? Have you never observed the sun rising on a calm morning? What majesty pervades, then, all Nature, when the variegated aspect of the heavens, when those mixed tinges of emerging light and vanishing shades, united with that diffusive pleasure issuing from the fecundated earth, exhibit the most august spectacle which this transitory life affords!

New York: E. P. Dutton, p. 550.

RELIGIOUS MEANING OF LAND: REVEREND
JOHN TODD'S *THE SUNSET LAND*

There were ranges back as far as you could see, but behind
the last range piled up against the sky there was a great unknown country.

The Red Pony, 52

In 1870 the Reverend John Todd published a glowing account of
his travels in California, attempting to interest citizens in settling
in the state. His positive description of California's vast and varied
resources served the cause of Manifest Destiny, the belief that the
United States had an almost holy destiny to acquire as much territory in the New World as possible by whatever means possible.
Todd consistently describes the California landscape in religious
terms. God has provided the resources and this beauty for mankind. God dwells in the beauty and plenty of the land. Like the
mountains that Jody and the old men who visit the ranch revere,
the spectacular features of the land lead Todd to the conclusion
that God must be present in such marvels as the Sierra Nevada,
the groves, the redwood forests, the Yosemite valleys and mountains, even the gold fields near Sacramento.

FROM JOHN TODD, *THE SUNSET LAND, OR, THE GREAT PACIFIC
SLOPE* (1870)

[I]rrigation must and will come into use more and more.
  Now, at the foot of the Sierra Nevada Mountains God has provided for
all this. There are over two hundred lakes and ponds, natural reservoirs,
where the waters are stored up,—enough to turn a vast territory into a
garden fair as Eden. (29, 30)

• • •

I have attempted, thus far, to help you to look over the landscape, and
see California as God made it. . . . In the vast and lofty mountains, in their
round, beautiful foothills, in the bewitching valleys, that sleep in beauty
through the country, in the peculiarity of climates, in the gorgeous drap-
ery of trees and flowers, in the sleeping gold and silver yet unfound, in
the fertility of soil and the great wealth yet to come from it, in its relations

to the Orient,—not yet touched upon,—I see a future for this part of our land, great in results, wide in their reach, fearful for good or for evil to the human family, but all, all under the orderings of a God infinite in wisdom. (36, 37)

. . .

Can we not see now that the discovery of gold on the Pacific slope evinces a strong evidence of an overruling Providence? There the precious metals were created and laid away in the dark, till the human family had migrated westward from their starting-point in Mesopotamia, till they had a new continent in their hands, till human civilization had advanced, till there was not a circulating medium to move its property and supply its wants, till the world was ready to leap up for a new race in human improvement; then the gold . . . flashed out of its dark hiding-place; and this continent has a new and an awful power for good or for evil, a power with which it may roll down woes on unborn generations, or by which it may bless all the families of the earth, and bring glory to God on earth, and deepen and multiply the anthems of heaven to all eternity. (74, 75)

. . .

Groves of Mariposa and Calaveras, farewell! We never before saw ages of time stamped upon a tree; never conceived in what forms greatness that awes, and grandeur that humbles, could be thus embodied; never before stood before living age so marvellous that one wanted to take off the hat, and look solemnly around, to see if the mighty Hand, that has so long upheld these wonders, is not now visibly upon them! (89)

. . .

The great impression which you receive on visiting this valley, is that man is small and God is great. We see here the foot-prints of his presence, and the finger-marks of his power; but *when* He was here, wonderful in working, *how* He chiseled out this wonderful spot! When the first rush of waters was heard, as they leaped down into this deep basin. (119, 120)

Boston: Lee and Shepard.

A GOLDEN EDEN: WASHINGTON IRVING'S
CAPTAIN BONNEVILLE

"Got a kitchen, orchard, cherries, apples, peaches,'cots, nuts, got a few berries."

Of Mice and Men, 57

Washington Irving's description of California as Captain Benjamin Louis Bonneville and his company found it in 1833 emphasizes the richness of California's natural resources, including the fertility of the oldest inhabited part of the region—the area around Monterey—which is precisely the setting of *The Red Pony* and *Of Mice and Men*. Irving's account of 1890 of the ability of the soil, climate, and availability of water to sustain agriculture and ranching in the area is consistent with the flourishing small ranch in *The Red Pony* and the large farm employing a large crew of workers in *Of Mice and Men*.

Bonneville, as well as others, returned to report the promise of farming successfully on uncharted land at a time, the 1830s, when Americans in the eastern United States were suffering from the effects of the 1827 economic crash, which had resulted in many workers losing their jobs and many farmers losing their land. California held out hope for the self-sufficiency that comes with ownership of land, and not just any land, but one rich beyond all imagination. Jody's childhood on the ranch has many of the qualities that Irving told prospective settlers that they would find. The climate, free of the bitter cold, snow, and ice of New England, helps sustain the Eden-like quality of Jody's early years. Likewise, the ease with which the climate and soil make self-sustenance possible (as described by Irving) feeds Lennie and George's dream of being able to take care of themselves on a little tract of land.

FROM WASHINGTON IRVING, *CAPTAIN BONNEVILLE* (1895)

They now turned towards the south, and passing numerous small bands of natives, posted upon various streams, arrived at the Spanish village and post of Monterey.

This is a small place, containing about two hundred houses, situated in latitude 37° north. It has a capacious bay, with indifferent anchorage. The surrounding country is extremely fertile, especially in the valleys; the soil is richer the further you penetrate into the interior, and the climate is described as a perpetual spring. Indeed, all California, extending along the Pacific Ocean from latitude 19° 30' [to] 42° north, is represented as one of the most fertile and beautiful in North America.

Lower California, in length about seven hundred miles, forms a great peninsula, which crosses the tropics and terminates in the torrid zone. . . . The peninsula is traversed by stern and barren mountains, and has many sandy plains, where the only sign of vegetation is the cylindrical cactus growing among the clefts of the rocks. Wherever there is water, however, and vegetable mould, the ardent nature of the climate quickens everything into astonishing fertility. There are valleys luxuriant with the rich and beautiful productions of the tropics. There the sugar-cane and indigo plant attain a perfection unequalled in any other part of North America. There flourish the olive, the fig, the date, the orange, the citron, the pomegranate, and other fruits belonging to the voluptuous climates of the south; with grapes in abundance, that yield a generous wine.

· · ·

The produce of the lands, and all the profits arising from sales, are entirely at the disposal of the priests; whatever is not required for the support of the mission, goes to augment a fund which is under their control. Hides and tallow constitute the principal riches of the missions, and, indeed, the main commerce of the country. Grain might be produced to an unlimited extent at the establishments, were there a sufficient market for it. Olives and grapes are also reared at the missions.

Horses and horned cattle abound throughout all this region; the former may be purchased at from three to five dollars, but they are of an inferior breed. Mules, which are here of a large size and of valuable qualities, cost from seven to ten dollars.

There are several excellent ports along this coast. San Diego, Santa Barbara, Monterey, the Bay of San Francisco, and the northern port of Bondago all afford anchorage for ships of the largest class. The port of San Francisco is too well known to require much notice in this place. The entrance from the sea is sixty-seven fathoms deep, and within, whole navies might ride with perfect safety. Two large rivers, which take their rise in mountains two or three hundred miles to the east, and run through a country unsurpassed for soil and climate, empty themselves into the harbor. The country around affords admirable timber for shipbuilding. In a word, this favored port combines advantages which not only fit it for a grand naval depot, but almost render it capable of being made the dominant military post of these seas. (98–104)

. . .

The arrival of supplies gave the regular finish to the annual revel. A grand outbreak of wild debauch ensued among the mountaineers—drinking, dancing, swaggering, gambling, quarrelling, and fighting. Alcohol, which, from its portable qualities, containing the greatest quantity of fiery spirit in the smallest compass, is the only liquor carried across the mountains, is the inflammatory beverage at these carousals, and is dealt out to the trappers at four dollars a pint. When inflamed by this fiery beverage, they cut all kinds of mad pranks and gambols, and sometimes burn all their clothes in their drunken bravadoes. A camp, recovering from one of these riotous revels, presents a serio-comic spectacle; black eyes, broken heads, lack-lustre visages. Many of the trappers have squandered in one drunken frolic the hard-earned wages of a year; some have run in debt, and must toil on to pay for past pleasure. All are sated with this deep draught of pleasure, and eager to commence another trapping campaign; for hardship and hard work, spiced with the stimulants of wild adventure, and topped off with an annual frantic carousal, is the lot of the restless trapper. (119–120)

New York: G. P. Putnam's Sons.

A GOLDEN EDEN: JOHN BIDWELL'S "THE FIRST EMIGRANT TRAIN TO CALIFORNIA"

"Every man wanted something for himself, but the big beast
that was all of them wanted only westering."
The Red Pony, 99

John Bidwell's party, comprising one of the first *groups* to go to California overland, set out in 1841, some eight years before the gold rush. This explanation of what attracted him to California is typical of the motivations of many who took the arduous trip west. He heard of this area by talking to someone who had made the trip earlier, a Frenchman named Roubideaux. Everything Bidwell learned painted the country as another Eden: the climate, the fertility of the land, the wild cattle and horses, the healthiness, and the attitude of the people. "His description of the country," Bidwell writes, "made it seem like a Paradise" (109). Many of Roubideaux's claims were corroborated by Bidwell's own experience once he reached California. Even though what the Spanish residents could offer these foreign pioneers was limited to meat and beans, they were generous, hospitable, and trusting, and around the missions Bidwell found the fruits of Paradise that one might have known about only from reading the Bible.

Even more than by the individual opportunities offered new settlers, these people, like Jody's grandfather, were motivated by "westering and westering" (*The Red Pony*, 99). And as Bidwell writes, after talking to Roubideaux, "I resolved to see that wonderful land" (109).

FROM JOHN BIDWELL, "THE FIRST EMIGRANT TRAIN TO
CALIFORNIA" (1890–1891)

The party whose fortunes I have followed across the plains was not only the first that went direct to California from the East; we were probably the first white people, except Bonneville's party of 1833, that ever crossed the Sierra Nevada. Dr. Marsh's ranch, the first settlement reached by us in California, was located in the eastern foothills of the Coast Range

Mountains, near the northwestern extremity of the great San Joaquin Valley and about six miles east of Monte Diablo, which may be called about the geographical center of Contra Costa County. There were not other settlements in the valley; it was, apparently, still just as new as when Columbus discovered America, and roaming over it were countless thousands of wild horses, of elk, and of antelope. . . . That valley was full of wild cattle,—thousands of them,—and they were more dangerous to one on foot, as I was, than grizzly bears.[1] (91, 92)

• • •

We had already heard that a man by the name of Sutter was starting a colony a hundred miles away to the north in the Sacramento Valley. No other civilized settlements had been attempted anywhere east of the coast Range; before Sutter came the Indians had reigned supreme. As the best thing to be done I now determined to go to Sutter's, afterward called "Sutter's Fort," or New Helvetia. Dr. Marsh said we could make the journey in two days, but it took us eight. Winter had come in earnest, and winter in California then, as now, meant rain. I had three companions. It was wet when we started, and much of the time we traveled through a pouring rain. Streams were out of their banks; gulches were swimming; plains were inundated; indeed, most of the country was overflowed. There were no roads, merely paths, trodden only by Indians and wild game. We were compelled to follow the paths, even when they were under water, for the moment our animals stepped to one side down they went into the mire. Most of the way was through the region now lying between Lathrop and Sacramento. We got out of provisions and were about three days without food. Game was plentiful, but hard to shoot in the rain. Besides, it was impossible to keep our old flint-lock guns dry, and especially the powder dry in the pans. On the eighth day we came to Sutter's settlement; the fort had not then been begun. Sutter received us with open arms and in a princely fashion, for he was a man of the most polite address and the most courteous manners, a man who could shine in any society. (93–94)

• • •

The kindness and hospitality of the native Californians have not been overstated. Up to the time the Mexican regime ceased in California they had a custom of never charging for anything; that is to say, for entertainment—food, use of horses, etc. You were supposed, even if invited to visit a friend, to bring your blankets with you, and one would be very thoughtless if he traveled and did not take a knife with him to cut his meat. When you had eaten, the invariable custom was to rise, deliver to the woman or hostess the plate on which you had eaten the meat and the beans—for that was about all they had—and say, *"Muchas gracias, Senora"* ("Many thanks, madame"); and the hostess as invariably replied, *"Buenas provecho"* ("May it do you much good"). The Missions in California invariably had gardens with grapes, olives, figs, pomegranates, pears, and apples, but the ranches scarcely ever had any fruit.[2] When you wanted a horse to ride, you would take it to the next ranch—it might be twenty, thirty, or fifty miles—and turn it out there, and sometime or other in reclaiming his stock the owner would get it back. In this way you might travel from one end of California to the other.

The ranch life was not confined to the country, it prevailed in the towns too. There was not a hotel in San Francisco, or Monterey, or anywhere in California, till 1846, when the Americans took the country. The priests at the Missions were glad to entertain strangers without charge. They would give you a room in which to sleep, and perhaps a bedstead with a hide stretched across it, and over that you could spread your blankets. (98–99)

• • •

But I still had in my mind to try the gold; so early in the spring of 1845 I made it a point to visit the mines in the south discovered by Ruelle in 1841. They were in the mountains about twenty miles north or northeast of the Mission of San Fernando, or say fifty miles from Los Angeles. I wanted to see the Mexicans working there, and to gain what knowledge I could of gold digging. Dr. John Townsend went with me. Pablo's confidence that there was gold on Bear Creek was fresh in my mind; and I hoped the same year to find time to return there and explore, and if possible find gold in the Sierra Nevada. (107)

• • •

It is a question whether the United States could have stood the shock of the great rebellion of 1861 had the California gold discovery not been made. Bankers and business men of New York in 1864 did not hesitate to admit that but for the gold of California, which monthly poured its six millions into that financial center, the bottom would have dropped out of everything. These timely arrivals so strengthened the nerves of trade and stimulated business as to enable the Government to sell its bonds at a time when its credit was its life-blood and the main reliance by which to feed, clothe, and maintain its armies. Once our bonds went down to thirty-eight cents on the dollar. California gold averted a total collapse, and enabled a preserved Union to come forth from the great conflict with only four billions of debt instead of a hundred billions. The hand of Providence so plainly seen in the discovery of gold is no less manifest in the time chosen for its accomplishments. (110–111)

• • •

In November or December of 1840, while still teaching school in Platt County, I came across a Frenchman named Roubideaux, who said he had been to California. He had been a trader in New Mexico, and had followed the road traveled by traders from the frontier of Missouri to Santa Fe. He had probably gone through what is now New Mexico and Arizona into California by the Gila River trail used by the Mexicans. His description of California was in the superlative degree favorable, so much so that I resolved if possible to see that wonderful land, and with others helped to get up a meeting at Weston and invited him to make a statement before it in regard to the country. At that time when a man moved out West, as soon as he was fairly settled he wanted to move again, and naturally every question imaginable was asked in regard to this wonderful country. Roubideaux described it as one of perennial spring and boundless fertility, and laid stress on the countless thousands of wild horses and cattle. He told about oranges, and hence must have been at Los Angeles, or the mission of San Gabriel, a few miles from it. Every conceivable question that we could ask him was answered favorably. Generally the first question which a Missourian asked about a country was whether there was any fever or ague. I remember his answer distinctly. He said there was but one man in California that had ever had a chill there, and it was a matter of so much wonderment to the people of Monterey that they went eighteen miles into the country to see him shake. Nothing could have been more satisfactory on the score of health. He said that the Spanish authorities were most friendly, and that the people were the most hospitable on the globe; that you could travel all over California and it would cost you nothing for horses or food. Even the Indians were friendly. His description of the country made it seem like a Paradise. . . . In a short time, I think within a month, we had about five hundred names; we also had correspondence on the subject with people all over Missouri, and even as far east as Illinois and Kentucky, and as far south as Arkansas. As soon as the movement was announced in the papers we had many letters of inquiry, and we expected people in considerable numbers to join us. About that time we heard of a man living in Jackson County, Missouri, who had received a letter from a person in California named Dr. Marsh, speaking favorably of the country, and a copy of this letter was published.

• • •

In those days Americans were held in disfavor by the native Californians on account of the war made by Americans in Texas to wrest Texas from Mexico. The number of Americans in California at this time was very small. When I went to California in 1841 all the foreigners—and all were foreigners except Indians and Mexicans—did not, I think, exceed one hundred; nor was the character of all of them the most prepossessing. Some had been trappers in the Rocky Mountains who had not seen civilization for a quarter of a century; others were men who had found their way into California, as Roubideaux had done, by way of Mexico; others still had gone down the Columbia River to Oregon and joined trapping parties in the service of the Hudson Bay Company going from Oregon to California—men who would let their beards grow down to their knees, and wear buckskin garments made and fringed like those of the Indians, and who considered it a compliment to be told "I took ye for an Injin." Another class of men from the Rocky Mountains were in the habit of making their way by the Mohave Desert south of the Sierra Nevada into California to steal horses, sometimes driving off four or five hundred at a time. The other Americans, most numerous perhaps, were sailors who had run away from vessels and remained in the country. With few exceptions this was the character of the American population when I came to California, and they were not generally a class calculated to gain much favor with the people. (115–117)

• • •

On leaving Weston, where there had been so much opposition, we were six or seven in number, and nearly half the town followed us for a mile, and some for five or six miles, to bid us good-by, showing the deep interest felt in our journey. All expressed good wishes and desired to hear from us. When we reached Sapling Grove, the place of rendezvous, in May, 1841, there was but one wagon ahead of us.

• • •

In five days after my arrival we were ready to start, but no one knew where to go, not even the captain. . . . Afterwards when we came in contact with Indians our people were so easily excited that if we had not had with us an old mountaineer the result would certainly have been disastrous. The name of the guide was Captain Fitzpatrick; he had been at the head of trapping parties in the Rocky Mountains for many years. (119)

1. The rancheros marked and branded their stock differently so as to distinguish them. But it was not possible to keep them separate. One would often steal cattle from the other. Livermore in this way lost cattle by his neighbor Amador. In fact it was almost a daily occurrence—a race to see which could get and kill the most of the other's cattle. Cattle in those days were often killed for the hides alone. One day a man saw Amador kill a fine steer belonging to Livermore. When he reached Livermore's—ten or fifteen miles away—and told him what Amador had done, he found Livermore skinning a steer of Amador's.

2. With the exception of the tuna, or prickly pear, these were the only culti-vated fruits I can recall to mind in California, except oranges, lemons, and limes, in a few places.

Century Illustrated Monthly Magazine 41 (November 1890–April 1891), 106–130.

A GOLDEN EDEN: REVEREND JOHN TODD'S *THE SUNSET LAND*

"The westering was as big as God . . ."

The Red Pony, 100

The Reverend Todd made his way to California during the gold rush days following 1849, and in 1869 first recorded his findings. Todd sees the hand of God in the California landscape, especially the dramatic mountains and gigantic redwoods. The religious meaning that the frontier holds for Todd is most clearly reflected in the stories "The Great Mountains" and "The Leader of the People" through the characters of Jody, the grandfather, and the old paisano, who sense the great spirit that dwells in the unexplored, especially the mountains.

However, Todd's diary reads more like a Chamber of Commerce pamphlet designed to attract settlers to the new area than a description of a religious experience. He justifies the scramble for gold and silver in California as high patriotism and seems to regard his selling of the idea of California as both a patriotic and a holy mission: "Can we not see now," he writes, "that the discovery of gold on the Pacific slope evinces a strong evidence of an overruling Providence? . . . which may bless all the families of the earth, and bring glory to God on earth, and deepen and multiply the anthems of heaven to all eternity" (75). Todd is more specific than earlier writers in describing exactly what opportunities exist for pioneers attracted to the state, especially in the area of farming. Because of California's special climate and soil, settlers could look forward to genuine self-sufficiency there. This foreshadows Lennie and George's dream of living off the fat of the land. They speak of keeping their own cows, pigs, and chickens, of catching and smoking their own salmon, and of canning fruit and vegetables raised on their own land.

FROM JOHN TODD, *THE SUNSET LAND, OR, THE GREAT PACIFIC SLOPE* (1870)

. . . It is of little consequence what a State is today, in comparison with the question, What is she to become?

In regard to California, her produce of today, either from soil or mines, in bushels, in tons, or in dollars, is of very little consequence, except as they bear on the future, and as they are an indication of what the plans of God are in the future, in regard to that territory.

We have no other State or section which has so great a variety of soil and climate as California, and no State which can yield such a *variety* of products. All that can be raised in the temperate zone, or in the semi-tropical climate, will grow here in the greatest profusion. The soil and climate are such that the same amount of labor will yield more than anywhere else, and of a quality unsurpassed. Instead of planting your seed and waiting years before you can eat your apple or your pear, you may feel sure of a good crop the third year. The rapidity of growth will astonish you, and not less, the early day at which you get returns. I saw in Oakland, in the garden of Mr. Hunt, formerly of Springfield, a large area of dwarf apple trees, none of which were much over two feet big, literally loaded with fruit, and off which his son assured me, that in the second year, they gathered apples which weighed twenty ounces each; and I saw, also, a limb of a fig tree, which he said he cut off the last fall and stuck into the ground, and which, this summer, is bearing figs. In the same garden is a century plant, whose stem was as large as a man's leg, and then, when I saw it, twenty-one feet high. It had grown fourteen feet in seven weeks. He predicted it would grow twenty feet more, and then blossom. How amazed we should be to see beets that will weigh one hundred and twenty-seven pounds each, onions a foot across the top, cabbages weighing eighty pounds each, and other vegetables in proportion! The great trouble there about fruit is, that, it is so easily raised, it has no market.

The first steamboat we entered on the Sacramento River had twelve tons of salmon, caught that day, and which she was carrying, as her daily allowance, to the city of San Francisco: the fish would weigh twenty pounds each, and they were retailing at six cents the pound, but can often be bought for twenty-five or thirty cents, the whole fish. The cars that come up from the Santa Clara valley, bring twelve tons of strawberries daily; and this fruit is in market every month in the year. The potato will yield at least two annual crops; and such huge potatoes! You can hardly persuade yourself that they were not at least four years in growing; the fig tree yields three crops. The long, dry summer allows the farmer to take his own time to harvest his wheat and his barley, and to let them lie in the field as long as he chooses. The mildness of the climate saves him the necessity of building barns or raising hay. He harvests his grains in the latter part of May, or the beginning of June; and one peculiarity is, that the dryness of the atmosphere causes the capsule of the wheat to contract and hold in the great plump kernel of wheat, or else there would be a great loss. The very thing which would shell out our wheat here, retains it there; so that, if your wheat stands uncut for two months after it is ripe, you sustain no loss. So you thresh it and put it into sacks in the field, and let it lie till convenient to carry it to market.

You know how, in our climate, immediately after a shower, the sun often pours down upon us, with heat almost insupportable. The reason is, the air is full of moisture. But in the valleys of California, where there is no rain or moisture, though the thermometer stands high, yet the heat causes no suffering—scarcely inconvenience. Another thing to be mentioned is the very superior quality of the wheat that grows there. There is nothing like it known in the world. They claim, too, that the great number of insectivorous birds, such as the beautiful valley-quail, protected by law, keep down the insect world. And the very dryness of the wheat, almost as if kiln-dried, preserves the berry well for exportation, and defends it from the weevil and other insects.

The average bushels of wheat to the acre, through the State, is less than it should be, from the fact, that it has been the fashion, after the first ploughing, which gives forty or fifty bushels to the acre, just to brush over the stubble, in the fall, with a bush-barrow, and trust that enough seed has been dropped to insure a crop. The ground was not probably moved an inch deep, and yet the second crop would be from twenty to twenty-five bushels to the acre. And so the third year, the crop would be from twelve to fifteen bushels. This system is exhaustive of the soil, and suicidal of the future; and this accounts for the low average per acre. They have been in the habit, too, of just clipping off the heads of the wheat and barley by a peculiar reaper, and then burning the stubble in the field. They are beginning to learn that this is poor economy, and are now ploughing in their stubble.

The annual produce of wheat, now, is about twenty bushels, and about half that amount in barley. This often yields, by the large field, eighty and even one hundred bushels to the acre. It is used chiefly for feed; for though Indian corn can be raised to great advantage, they find the barley better feed in their climate, and much more easily raised. Of oats they raise two millions of bushels, of superior quality; but this is not a favorite crop.

To show you on what a scale things may be and are done by our friends there, I would state, that Mr. Jones, on his ranch, in the neighborhood of Stockton, in San Joaquin valley, has, this year, sixteen thousand acres of wheat; to prepare the ground for which, he had nine hundred horses ploughing at the same time; thus, calling his yield but half a crop, he will have three hundred and twenty thousand bushels of wheat, and that the cost of the sacks to put it in will be thirty thousand dollars: that a Mr. Hathaway raised twenty-one tons of beets on an acre, among which was one beet that weighed one hundred and seven pounds: that the same gentleman also gathered one hundred and thirty-two bushels of oats from an acre: that General Bidwell, in one year, raised thirty thousand acres of grain. (125–132)

• • •

From what has been said, you cannot doubt that California is to be, at some future time, like the garden of the Lord. There are sixty-five millions of acres of land that can be cultivated and made most productive; while there are thirty-three or thirty-four millions of acres,—about one third of the whole State,—which is too mountainous to be cultivated.

There are only a little over four hundred thousand people there yet, to occupy it, and nearly half of these are in the city of San Francisco. Only seven per cent. of the land is yet fenced in at all, and not over three per cent. is cultivated. When the ninety-seven parts remaining shall be cultivated, what may it not produce? A short time since it was thought that wheat would grow only in the rich valleys. But over the hills, and far up too, grows a little bush, called the "Tar Bush," with a beautiful leaf; but it sticks to and defiles whatever touches it. Hence its name. But it is found that wherever the "tar bush" grows, the soil is suitable for wheat.

Eastern mind, and skill, and perseverance, will meet ample reward. My traveling companion met a Massachusetts gentleman, who, seven years ago, bought his lands for one dollar per acre, and last year produced twenty thousand gallons of wine, two hundred thousand cocoons, has fifty thousand vines, and a garden filled with fruits. Lower California has a climate that never freezes, and the thermometer seldom rises, even in summer, higher than 65° or 70°. I know of no climate in the world more beautiful, and no region so inviting to enterprise as that. (139–141)

• • •

At first, nobody expected to stay in California only long enough to find gold; nobody thought the soil capable of producing anything. So that it was not till about eleven years ago that men felt safe to go into manufacturing; and so much afraid were they of dishonesty in companies, that it is said two thirds of all the manufacturing done in the State is done by less than one hundred owners. The nearness to China and Japan has done much to stimulate machine-shops and mills for rolling iron. At the time when the commerce of the world is increasing beyond all precedent, God is opening new sources of industry. Ship timber is becoming scarce on the Atlantic coast; but go north of California, and there is Puget Sound, unequalled for timber, where ships can be built better, and stronger, and cheaper than anywhere else in our country, or in the world; and where, not unlikely, within a very short time, the ship-building of this continent will be transferred and carried on, and whence, every ship, for any part of the world, can start loaded with lumber. (143–144)

• • •

I have thus given a bird's-eye view of the capabilities of California—where nothing that man has done is over twenty years old,—and yet he has achieved wonders,—where the hand of man has yet touched but three per cent. of her rich soil, where everything is and grows, and is to be and grow, on a scale unexampled, and where the invitations for men to go are loud. But the men to go there should be men of industry, men of intelligence, men who only want opportunity and materials with which to work, and if they can carry capital, so much the better; but it is not the place for drones, or those who want to live without labor. Such are not welcomed; but the right kind of men are welcomed with a cordiality that is beautiful.

The inhabitants gathered there are from all parts of the world, and they all understand that they are to lay aside their prejudices, and melt into a new and homogeneous society; and they do so.

The country is a new field for human industry, and experiments new and great are there to be made. God has reserved all this for designs which I shall hint at hereafter.

Mines of the precious metals there are, and mines of iron, and lead, and copper, and quicksilver; mines of coal and tin there are; but after all, the deep, rich soil of the State will be the great source of wealth, and will call in a population that will carry there all that is good in the old States, leaving behind, I trust, what is evil.

I stand on the Nevadas, and look off over this country; and I am not looking at so many acres of grain, so many mines, so many factories, but I am looking at a territory now embraced in a single State, which, when filled up as Massachusetts is today, will contain twenty millions of people,—where generation after generation is to come up and pass away,—where art, and mind, and wealth, and skill, and luxury, and ambition, and education, and religion will all struggle together for supremacy, but through it all, will roll the River of God to make glad the cities of our God, and to cool the passions, and moderate the spirits, and fit the unborn multitudes for a higher end than can be attained on any, even the most favored spot, in this world. (157–160)

Boston: Lee and Shepard.

NOTE

1. Quoted in Andrew F. Rolle, *California: A History* (New York: Thomas Y. Crowell, 1969), p. 352.

TOPICS FOR WRITTEN OR ORAL EXPLORATION

1. What frontiers are left to explore in the final decades of the twentieth century?

2. Write an essay defining "Eden."

3. Write an essay on nineteenth-century California as Eden.

4. Using as many sources as you can, write an essay on the meaning of gold.

5. Carefully analyze the relationship of Carl Tiflin and his father-in-law. What do you suppose is behind Carl's disgust with the old man?

6. Explain why Billy Buck and the grandfather have high regard for one another.

7. Construct a map showing the locations referred to in *The Red Pony* and *Of Mice and Men*.

8. Construct a map showing the trails, major mining camps, towns, and forts in California in the 1840s and 1850s.

9. Find and report on the gold mining towns that still exist in California. Are they all ghost towns?

10. Write an essay comparing and contrasting George and Lennie's dream of land with the forty-niners' quest for gold.

11. The grandfather in *The Red Pony* says, essentially, that the questing or the traveling is more important than the goal or destination reached. Can you apply this sentiment to other things?

12. Steinbeck and several nineteenth-century writers quoted above were interested in the character of all-male societies and their effect on individuals. Can you think of any all-male societies that exist today? If so, do they have any characteristics in common with those you have read about in this chapter?

13. Keeping in mind the reports in this chapter, have a debate about the inclusion of females in formerly all-male groups such as the military and certain universities.

14. Write an essay on the subject of women in both the memoirs of old California and in *Of Mice and Men*.

15. In *Of Mice and Men* and the memoirs of old California, to what extent is it implied that the family is a civilizing agency? Why is this true?

16. Have a roundtable discussion on why the move west tended to erase a sense of personal history. Consider this issue as it arises in *The Red*

Pony and in *Of Mice and Men*. In what sense is this positive? In what sense is it negative?

SUGGESTIONS FOR FURTHER READING

Billington, Ray A. *Westward Expansion* (New York: Macmillan, 1949).

Branch, Douglas D. *Westward: The Romance of the American Frontier* (New York: Appleton, 1930).

Burton, Richard F. *The City of the Saints* and *Across the Rocky Mountains to California* (New York: Harper Brothers, 1861).

Clark, Thomas D. *Frontier America: The Story of the Westward Movement* (New York: Scribners, 1959).

Handlin, Oscar. *This Was America* (Cambridge: Harvard University Press, 1949).

Howard, Robert W. *This Is the West* (Chicago: Rand McNally, 1957).

Rolle, Andrew F. *California: A History* (New York: Crowell, 1969).

Roosevelt, Theodore. *The Winning of the West* (New York: G. P. Putnam's Sons, 1889–1896).

Royce, Sarah. *A Frontier Lady* (New Haven: Yale University Press, 1932).

Stewart, George R. *The California Trail* (Lincoln: University of Nebraska Press, 1962).

Tryon, W. S., ed. *Mirror for Americans* (Chicago: University of Chicago Press, 1959).

Webb, Walter Prescott. *The Great Plains* (Boston: Ginn & Co., 1931).

3

Land Ownership

Land was always an essential part of the American Dream, and it is an idea central to both *The Red Pony* and *Of Mice and Men*, but in very different ways. Steinbeck takes several approaches to the concept of land in these novellas. In *The Red Pony* the interest is in the landscape as nature, but also in the spirit inherent in the land, what one might call its religious meaning and its connection to the idea of the Garden of Eden. In *Of Mice and Men*, while there are still strong connections to the Garden of Eden, the approach must be labeled more social than religious. That is, the land is in this instance tied more to the politics of this world than to the mystery of the next world.

The constant presence of the land—the natural place or setting—in the fiction is nowhere so pervasive in Steinbeck's work as in *The Red Pony*. The reader becomes familiar with the details of the farm itself—the spring, the edge of the yard, the killing tree, the chicken yard, the barn, the corral, the road. Even the distant land that surrounds the farm is a powerful presence. This comprises the mountains and the paths Jody takes home from school and from a neighboring ranch. Nowhere in the four stories of *The Red Pony* does Jody or the reader escape the land by moving into a town, village, or city. One sees the various faces of the landscape—spring and summer, fall and winter, rain and sunshine.

Gold seekers on their way to the mines. A drawing from the 1850s by Charles Nahl.

And the creatures supported by the land on which Jody lives—horses, pigs, dogs, chickens, vultures, various other birds, and mice—form an integral part of it. These, rather than a cast of villagers, are the characters in *The Red Pony*.

All of the human characters in this novella live intimately with nature—the land—and one of the main themes is Jody's changing relationship to the natural world, shown graphically in his interaction with the horses and his defiance of the vultures.

In the beginning, the ranch is a kind of Garden of Eden and Jody a young Adam who has been put in charge of the animals, specifically the dogs, the chickens, and his pony. Even though the ranch is isolated, however, brutality intrudes, and Jody and the reader begin to feel that nature is not always golden and Eden-like. Even the beautiful land Jody lives on is fallen and flawed.

Land is physical nature in the novella, but it also embodies spirit. It is part and parcel of God. This is especially true of land unadulterated by man. In this novella, spirit or God resides in the mountains. Like God, the mountains are majestic and unknowable, even somewhat frightening, yet full of meaning that Jody can sense but not explain. They beckon to Jody and to Gitano, the old man who knows he is facing death. In a place where death or mortality has made itself so apparent on the surface in the deaths of the pony, Nellie, and the pigs, both Jody and Gitano look beyond and behind the land for the immortality of the spirit, that which lives even after the body dies. The religious meaning behind the land is most obvious in Gitano who, like many Native Americans, feels that his birth on the land near Jody's house identifies him with and bonds him to that site. In summary, *The Red Pony* is an affirmation of the religious character of land as a bestower of meaning. The universality of this idea can be seen in the work of twentieth-century advocates of land reform, who note that South American people refer to the spiritual meaning of land in something of the same way that the Hebrew scriptures do. Roy H. May, Jr., writes: "Land always is simultaneously literal and symbolic. It signifies physical and existential well-being and security."[1]

In *Of Mice and Men*, land, which is synonymous with home and family, assumes tremendous importance as well, but more from a social than a religious point of view. Men like Lennie and George have been dispossessed of land for so long that they can't remember when they ever had a home. Like the poor migrants sailing to the New World and the pioneers traveling to the American West, the land is not essentially part of their lived past, their remembered history. It is, rather, a dream of the future, of an impossible Eden. The idea of an Edenic life on one's own land opens *Of Mice and Men* in a description of a willow-bound pool in the foothills of the majestic mountains. This description, with its use of the color gold and the sense of harmony has an almost dreamlike quality.

At the same time, Lennie and George's plan to own their own farm is a dream of a return to Eden where they can "live offa the fat of the lan' " (14). The farm dream, with its rabbits and chickens and vegetable patch, is an idyllic one of ideal independence and freedom. As in Eden, they will be free there from the back-breaking labor to which they now travel, going from farm to farm. George explains to Slim that the dream is one of independence and the satisfaction of reaping his own crops.

George's third incantation of the land dream, just before Candy joins in, echoes the Eden-like portrayal of California missions sent back east in the early 1840s.

That Eden in reality is sullied is signaled with Lennie's return to the pond, where there is now a "shadow in the valley" (105). A shade has fallen over the scene, and a serpent, Biblical symbol of evil, glides over it. The destructiveness emerges in Eden as a heron devours the snake. No sooner has this snake been devoured, however, than another appears.

The story of George and Lennie's dream of land is, of course, the American Dream of self-sufficiency, plenty, and freedom. That story begins in America with the settling of the New World by England and Europe's poor. There was not even the remotest possibility in the Old World for most of the poor to have the freedom and respect that come with land ownership. They were doomed always to live on and work someone else's land, as are Lennie and George. Only with the opening up of a New World to these emigrants—a New World often described as Eden—was there a possibility of a decent life. While the plans of many, like those of George and Lennie, were doomed to failure, others found what they were seeking—a plot of land by means of which they secured not only an independent subsistence, but personal esteem in the eyes of the world.

The vastness of the continent, unsettled by Europeans, allowed the founders of the United States to find a persistent theme in the *right* of every citizen to own land. To advance such an argument, they had to prevent the Old World system of land distribution from taking hold, whereby a very few monopolized vast tracts of land, leaving nothing for most people to call their own. The European system did take hold in the South, where huge plantations developed, and in the Southwest, where a few men received large grants from the Spanish government. (In the nineteenth century one such grant was given to John Sutter, the man on whose land gold was discovered in California.) To prevent such a practice from becoming widespread at the time of the nation's founding, Thomas Paine and Thomas Jefferson, in particular, turned to the philosophy of John Locke to define exactly how one can own land. In Locke's view, the earth was meant by God to be held in common by all people. And the only way one could rightfully appropriate a tract of land was to mix one's own labor with it—not the labor of someone else who was either enslaved or hired. So an untilled field could not be yours until you yourself had ploughed and planted it. The amount of land that one could rightfully appropriate was also, of course, at issue. That amount, according to Locke, was determined by the amount that you could actually till and the production from it that the owner could actually use. That portion of land which produced more than an owner could use could not by right be claimed by him. So a plantation that produced acres and acres of cotton, much more than the owner could use to make clothes for himself and his family, could not by right belong to him. Using this definition, there would always be enough for everyone to till a plot of his own and not be consigned to work for someone else and be at someone else's mercy. The political philosophy which discouraged the appropriation by a relative few of large tracts of land was the cornerstone of democracy which, it was argued, would foster greater equality among the citizens of the new, land-rich country.

In 1787 Congress established offices to help individuals secure plots of land. Eventually a tax structure was put in place that encouraged broad individual land ownership.

The quest for one's own land was the driving force behind settlement of the country beyond the East Coast, the pioneers first pushing into the Mississippi Valley beyond the Appalachian Mountains and with each decade pushing further and further west, eventually reaching the fertile, uncharted farmlands of California.

Like Jefferson and Paine in the eighteenth century, many nine-teenth-century thinkers believed that the hunger to own land was a fundamental urge, and that everyone had a right to inde-pendence and the pursuit of happiness that came with land own-ership. Furthermore, they believed that the fate of democracy would be determined by a fair distribution of land. Only those who own land, they would argue, believe that they have a real stake in the future of the country, and only they will act respon-sibly in determining its fate. To encourage responsible and wide-spread participation in government, a number of public figures urged people who were being ill-used by urban industries to fol-low the western horizon in pursuit of their own land, all of which, one has to remember, actually belonged to Indians native to America.

Making land available to every citizen was a crucial matter in the nineteenth century. As a result of this concern, in 1844 land re-formers, the Workingman's Party of New York, the National Reform Association, and the Spartan Band, formed their own organization with the express purpose of establishing the right of every person to land. In 1845 they supported political candidates sympathetic to their cause with the rallying cry, "Vote Yourself a Farm!" In order to provide land for the homeless, the new organization urged government to "limit the quantity of land that anyone may henceforth monopolize and inherit; and to make the public lands free to actual settlers only, each having the right to sell his im-provements to any man not possessed of land."[2]

Laws were passed in the nineteenth century to encourage family-sized farms: five different "Pre-emption Acts" in the 1830s were designed to allow people who settled on unoccupied land without benefit of titles—"squatters," they were called—to remain and purchase property at the low rate of $1.25 an acre.

However, in California especially, determining just who owned land was extremely difficult. Many of the social problems in nine-teenth-century California were seen as being caused by the incon-clusiveness of land titles. The Mexican government had given titles to California land to many of its citizens long before the area was ceded to the United States. In a few cases these titles were exces-sive, far exceeding what any one family could remotely till and use. In the great majority of cases, however, the acreage given to the Spanish and Mexican Californios was reasonable. Things changed drastically when California became a state and the gold rush and other enticements drew huge numbers of pioneers from the other states. Many of these people began squatting on the land owned by the Californios and tried to acquire titles themselves. John Sutter, a Swiss on whose extensive land gold was discovered, found himself in the ironic position of losing almost all his vast holdings as squatters confiscated his land. Heated arguments were presented on both sides of the question, and any title to land in California remained dubious and subject to challenge for most of the nineteenth century.

Despite the philosophy about land ownership espoused by the founding fathers in the eighteenth century, forces were at work from the time of the nation's birth to undermine the right of every citizen to own land. Land speculators moved in to claim thousands of unoccupied acres to sell at higher prices than they had paid for them. Eastern colonies and then states extended their western borders indefinitely to claim ownership of unsettled land as their own.

While large plantations were an integral part only of the Southern system of agriculture before the Civil War, afterwards there was an ever escalating tendency for large farms and then corporate farms to take over smaller family farms. California had also had massive spreads of land belonging to only a few landowners. In 1871, for example, 516 men in California owned 8,685,439 acres of land. In Fresno County 48 owners each had over 79,000 acres. Sixteen people in California controlled 84 square miles of the land. As examples of what might be called excessive land ownership, one railroad magnate managed to claim 400,000 acres of land for his private use; one state surveyor claimed 350,000 acres of land for his private use; and another state surveyor claimed 300,000 for his private use—all at rock bottom prices. In 1870, 1/500 of the California population owned half or more of the agricultural land. By 1940 these huge estates were still largely intact.

On these massive spreads, the actual work was done not by the owners, but by hired hands. Consider the situation in *Of Mice and Men*, where the owners, Curley and his father, give evidence that they are not working men by wearing high-heeled boots and spurs.

As the twentieth century wore on, fewer and fewer people owned more and more of the farmland. At mid-century, just 3 percent of the United States population owned all of the farmland. John Hart, author of *The Spirit of the Earth*, writes: "Such startling figures, unknown to most Americans and with unpleasant implications for *all* Americans, contradict the American dream and the American heritage."[3]

The opportunity for individual farmers to own modest tracts of land had almost from the first been especially limited in California, despite the promises to pioneers in the early days. The gold rush had given large producers instant markets in the cities and mining camps, and the railroads had made mass marketing of produce attractive to large corporations. Even by the end of the nineteenth century, most of California's crops were produced on comparatively few very large farms with absentee ownership. By the 1930s, when Lennie and George were bindle stiffs working their way from farm to farm and longing for their own land, California agriculture was already in the hands of the agribusinesses that would threaten small farms in the Midwest much later.

To Lennie and George and the rest of these migrant farm workers, the American Dream means owning a little bit of land. Their inability to be landowners means that they can never achieve independence, self-support, or the American Dream. The documents that follow reveal the American concern with land ownership as a cornerstone of democracy. They assert the right of every citizen to own land, discuss the effect of land ownership on character, and describe attempts to make land ownership more equitable. Also included is an assessment of just how far the American Dream had been diluted by massive agribusinesses by the 1940s.

John Steinbeck, in a series of articles written in 1937 on the problem of landless and homeless farm workers in California, suggested that the best solution was to find some way to put land in the hands of farm workers. One has to think of the dream of Lennie and George and the other ranch hands in considering Steinbeck's solution:

> Since the greatest number of the white American migrants are former farm owners, renters or laborers, it follows that their training and ambition have never been removed from agriculture. It is suggested that lands be leased; or where it is possible, that state and Federal lands be set aside as subsistence farms for migrants. These can be leased at a low rent or sold on long time payments to families

of migrant workers. . . . People who take these farms should be encouraged and helped to produce for their own subsistence fruits, vegetables and livestock—pigs, chickens, rabbits, turkeys and ducks.[4]

THE RIGHT TO LAND: THOMAS PAINE'S
"AGRARIAN JUSTICE"

"Old things ought to be put out of their misery."
The Red Pony, 49

"I am Gitano, and I have come back. . . . Back to the rancho.
I was born here, and my father, too."
The Red Pony, 44

In an essay entitled "Agrarian Justice," Thomas Paine, a political influence on the American war for independence and the establishment of the new nation, followed John Locke in arguing that land belongs to all people in common in the natural state. Civilization and cultivation have led to inequities, however, such that some people own great amounts of land which is passed down to their heirs for centuries, while others own nothing. Those who have no land, he writes, have been dispossessed of their part of the land which the creator intended all men to hold in common. Furthermore, certain classes of people—the blind, the lame, and the aged poor—live in wretchedness. One is reminded of the old paisano in *The Red Pony* and Candy, Crooks, and the retarded Lennie in *Of Mice and Men.* It is ironic that Paine himself, who had actually been given a great tract of land by the new government of the United States, died in abject poverty and was buried in a pauper's grave on that land.

To create capital to relieve the poverty of those who have been dispossessed of their land as well as those who are unable to help themselves, Paine proposes that a substantial portion of the estate of any person who dies be left to the state. These funds would be used to relieve the suffering of the landless poor, who, he contends, have been dispossessed of rightful ownership.

The entire text of "Agrarian Justice" shows Paine's proposal to be far ahead of its time, perhaps only beginning to be realized in the time of Steinbeck's stories with the establishment of Social Security and the New Deal under Franklin Roosevelt.

FROM THOMAS PAINE, "AGRARIAN JUSTICE" (1797)

It is a position not to be controverted that the earth, in its natural un-cultivated state was, and ever would have continued to be, *the common property of the human race*. In that state everyman would have been born to property. He would have been a joint life proprietor with the rest in the property of the soil, and in all its natural productions, vege-table and animal.

But the earth in its natural state, as before said, is capable of supporting but a small number of inhabitants compared with what it is capable of doing in a cultivated state. And as it is impossible to separate the im-provement made by cultivation from the earth itself, upon which that improvement is made, the idea of landed property arose from that insep-arable connection.

· · ·

There could be no such thing as landed property originally. Man did not make the earth, and, though he had a natural right to *occupy* it, he had no right to *locate as his property* in perpetuity any part of it; neither did the creator of the earth open a land-office, from whence the first title-deeds should issue. Whence then, arose the idea of landed property? I answer as before, that when cultivation began the idea of landed property began with it, from the impossibility of separating the improvement made by cultivation from the earth itself, upon which that improvement was made. The value of the improvement so far exceeded the value of the natural earth, at that time, as to absorb it, till, in the end, the common right of all became confounded into the cultivated right of the individual. But there are, nevertheless, distinct species of rights, and will continue to be so long as the earth endures.

It is only by tracing things to their origin that we can gain rightful ideas of them, and it is by gaining such ideas that we discover the boundary that divides right from wrong, and teaches every man to know his own. I have entitled this tract Agrarian Justice, to distinguish it from Agrarian Law. Nothing could be more unjust than Agrarian Law in a country im-proved by cultivation; for though every man, as an inhabitant of the earth, is a joint proprietor of it in its natural state, it does not follow that he is a joint proprietor of cultivated earth. The additional value made by cul-tivation, after the system was admitted, became the property of those who did it, or who inherited it from them, or who purchased it. It had origi-nally no owner. Whilst, therefore, I advocate the right, and interest myself in the hard case of all those who had been thrown out of their natural inheritance by the introduction of the system of landed property, I equally defend the right of the possessor to the part which is his.

Cultivation is at least one of the greatest natural improvements ever made by human invention. It has given to created earth a tenfold value. But the landed monopoly that began with it has produced the greatest evil. It has dispossessed more than half the inhabitants of every nation of their natural inheritance, without providing for them, as ought to have been done, an indemnification for that loss, and has thereby created a species of poverty and wretchedness that did not exist before.

In advocating the case of the persons thus dispossessed, it is a right, and not a charity, that I am pleading for. But it is that kind of right which, being neglected at first, could not be brought forward afterwards till heaven had opened the way by a revolution in the system of government. Let us then do honour to revolutions by justice, and give currency to their principles by blessings.

Having thus in a few words, opened the merits of the case, I shall now proceed to the plan I have to propose, which is,

To create a National Fund, out of which there shall be paid to every person, when arrived at the age of twenty-one years, the sum of fifteen pounds sterling, as a compensation in part, for the loss of his or her natural inheritance, by the introduction of the system of landed property:

And also, the sum of ten pounds per annum, during life, to every person now living, of the age of fifty years, and to all others as they shall arrive at that age.

Middletown, N.J.: George H. Evans.

THE RIGHT TO LAND: HECTOR ST. JOHN DE CREVECOEUR'S *LETTERS FROM AN AMERICAN FARMER*

"We could live offa the fatta the lan'. "

Of Mice and Men, 57

In this second excerpt from Crevecoeur, this time from his *Letters from an American Farmer*, he argues that the New World is a paradise for many of Europe's poor because here they can own their own land. Here they escape the traditions and inequities that have put inherited lands in the hands of a few. Here are available unknown, vast, tracts of land and the opportunity for even the poorest eventually to possess their own ground and enjoy the freedom that only self-sufficiency brings.

FROM HECTOR ST. JOHN DE CREVECOEUR, *LETTERS FROM AN AMERICAN FARMER* (1912)

The instant I enter on my own land, the bright idea of property, of exclusive right, of independence exalts my mind. Precious soil, I say to myself, by what singular custom of law is it that thou wast made to constitute the riches of the freeholder? What should we American farmers be without the distinct possession of that soil? It feeds, it clothes us, from it we draw even a great exuberancy, our best meat, our richest drink, the very honey of our bees comes from this privileged spot. No wonder we should thus cherish its possession, no wonder that so many Europeans who have never been able to say that such portion of land was theirs, cross the Atlantic to realize that happiness. This formerly rude soil has been converted by my father into a pleasant farm, and in return it has established all our rights; on it is founded our rank, our freedom, our power as citizens, our importance as inhabitants of such a district. These images I must confess I always behold with pleasure, and extend them as far as my imagination can reach: for this is what may be called the true and the only philosophy of an American farmer.

• • •

In this great American asylum, the poor of Europe have by some means met together, and in consequence of various causes; and to what purpose should they ask one another what countrymen they are? Alas, two thirds of them had no country. Can a wretch who wanders about, who works and starves, whose life is a continual scene of sore affliction or pinching penury; can that man call England or any other kingdom his country? . . . The laws, the indulgent laws, protect them as they arrive, stamping on them the symbol of adoption; they receive rewards for their labors; these accumulated rewards procure them lands; those lands confer on them the title of freemen, and to that title every benefit is affixed which men can possibly acquire.

• • •

Europe contains hardly any other distinctions but lords and tenants; this fair country alone is settled by freeholders, the possessors of the soil they cultivate.

London: J. M. Dent and Sons, pp. 66–80.

LAND OWNERSHIP AND CHARACTER IN CALIFORNIA: JOSIAH ROYCE'S *CALIFORNIA: A STUDY OF AMERICAN CHARACTER*

"I never seen a guy really do it," he said. "I seen guys nearly crazy with loneliness for land, but ever' time a whore house or a blackjack game took what it takes."

Of Mice and Men, 76

By the 1840s and 1850s California had become a focus for those seeking land in Eden—a place where they believed there were great tracts of uncultivated land which, at the same time, held the promise of being especially fertile, in a good growing climate with water easily available. But obstacles lay in the way of having one's own land to cultivate. Ironically, land ownership was the most momentous controversy in nineteenth-century California, where George and Lennie's story of a dream of land ownership takes place. Philosopher-historian Josiah Royce enlarges on this problem and its implications for the American character. The early controversy over land titles in California arose from the awarding of tracts—in some instances, huge tracts—of land by the Mexican government before California became part of the United States. After it was admitted as a state, settlers from the East flooded into the area and attempted to acquire land for cultivation by squatting on land that appeared to be unoccupied, whereas in reality many of the squatters were settling on land that had already been deeded to the native Californios by Mexico. Not only did this create acrimony between the newcomers and the natives, but it made all land deeds uncertain and unstable. It also led to widespread criminal activity on both sides—on the part of the original owners of large tracts who had been dispossessed of land that was legally theirs, and on the part of the pioneers who confiscated what was not legally theirs. The result was, as Royce points out, social unrest and continual vagrancy, so that few settlers felt they had a stake in the well-being and advancement of the state.

FROM JOSIAH ROYCE, *CALIFORNIA: A STUDY OF AMERICAN
CHARACTER* (1886)

Early Land-Troubles

How significant all this must be for the future of the State, is evident at
a glance. The future California must needs be an agricultural province,
whatever the gold excitement might for the time make the country see.
And that its land titles should soon be settled, and in an honest way, was
an essential of all true progress. . . . Doubt, insecurity, retarded progress,
litigation without end, hatred, destruction of property, bloodshed,—all
these have resulted for us from the fact that we tried as much as we did
to defraud these Californians of the rights that we guaranteed to them at
the moment of the conquest. And in the end, with all our toil, we escaped
not from the net, and it binds our land-seekers still.

• • •

[B]y the winter of 1849 there were enough landless, idle, and disappointed wanderers present in Sacramento to make the existence of land
ownership thereabouts appear to these persons as an intolerable burden,
placed upon the necks of the poor by rapacious land-speculators. Such
reflections are, of course, the well-known expression of human avarice
and disappointment everywhere in the world. Here they assumed, however, a new and dangerous form. One asked, "How comes it that there
is any ownership of land in this golden country at all? Is this not a free
land? Is it not our land? Is not the public domain free to all American
citizens?" The very simple answer was, of course, that this land was not
public domain. . . .

• • •

It is not to be wondered at that, under these circumstances, the Californians—who had never been exactly moral heroes—rapidly tended towards the utter degradation in which we have always meanly declared
them to have been placed by nature.

But as for us, who thus sought to despoil by legal means those whom
we were too orderly to rob on any grand scale by violence, we could not
altogether escape from the demoralization that we tried to inflict.

• • •

From the first moment of the conquest until the end of these early days
we showed how we were come to this land to get ourselves our own

private enjoyments; but we also showed how we thereby did get for ourselves nothing so much as public calamities. To this continual petty disorder there was indeed at last a relief. The greater claims being decided, the more serious quarrels ended, the State was at length free, in the years since 1870, to develop far more rapidly her material and moral resources, to attract a large new population, and to cultivate the arts of civilization. Yet even to-day one hears occasionally of the old sort of land-quarrel, with its brutal and sometimes bloody consequences. And meanwhile, if one complains of the unfortunate concentration of the land in a comparatively few hands, of the lack of small proprietors in certain parts of the State, and of the evils attendant upon such a state of things, one has to remember that these evils also are in great part a result of the policy which, instead of encouraging the old Californians to sell their grants in small tracts to new-comers, forced them at length to part with their lands in vast tracts to their lawyers, or to scheming speculators, so that these profited by the misfortunes of the Californians, to the lasting injury of the whole State.

• • •

The race that has since grown up in California, as the outcome of these early struggles, is characterized by very marked qualities of strength and weakness, some of which, perchance, even a native Californian like the author, who neither can nor would outgrow his healthy local traits, may still be able to note and confess. A general sense of social irresponsibility is, even to-day, the average Californian's easiest failing. Like his father, he is probably a born wanderer, who will feel as restless in his farm life, or in his own town, as his father felt in his. . . . He is apt to lack a little, moreover, complete devotion to the life within the household, because, as people so often have out, the fireside, an essential institution of our English race, is of such small significance in the climate of California. In short, the Californian has too often come to love mere fullness of life, and to lack reverence for the relations of life.

Boston: Houghton Mifflin, pp. 467–501.

EQUITY AND LAND OWNERSHIP: THE HOMESTEAD ACT OF 1862

The Homestead Act of 1862 was one of numerous legislative acts that sought to promote the American Dream of land ownership. It was preceded in the 1830s by five Pre-emption Acts which allowed citizens to establish themselves on public lands and to buy at cheap prices the land they had staked out. The Homestead Act allowed any adult citizen or would-be citizen to acquire as much as 160 acres free of charge, provided they had resided on the land for five years. Or the prospective landowner could acquire the land with only a six-months' residency by paying $1.25 an acre for it.

FROM THE HOMESTEAD ACT OF 1862

May 20, 1862. Chap. LXXV.—An Act to secure Homesteads to actual Settlers on the Public Domain *Be it enacted by the Senate and the House of Representatives of the United States of America in Congress Assembled*, That any person who is the head of a family, or who has arrived at the age of twenty-one years, and is a citizen of the United States, or who shall have filed his declaration of intention to become such, as required by the naturalization laws of the United States, and who has never borne arms against the United States Government or given aid and comfort to its enemies, shall, from and after the first January, eighteen hundred and sixty-three, be entitled to enter one quarter section or a less quantity of unappropriated public lands, upon which said person may have filed a preemption claim, or which may at the time the application is made, be subject to preemption at one dollar and twenty-five cents, or less, per acre; or eighty acres or less of such unappropriated lands, at two dollars and fifty cents per acre, to be located in a body, in conformity to the legal subdivisions of the public lands, and after the same shall have been surveyed: *Provided*, That any person owning and residing on land may, under the provisions of this act, enter other land lying contiguous to his or her said land, which shall not, with the land so already owned and occupied, exceed in the aggregate one hundred and sixty acres.

Sec. 2. *And be it further enacted*, That the person applying for the benefit of this act shall, upon application to the register of the land office in which he or she is about to make such entry, make affidavit before the said register or receiver that he or she is the head of a family, or is twenty-one years or more of age, or shall have performed service in the army or navy of the United States . . . and that such application is made for his or her exclusive use and benefit, and that said entry is made for the purpose of actual settlement and cultivation, and not either directly or indirectly for the use or benefit of any other person or persons whomsoever; and upon filing the said affidavit with the register or receiver, and on payment of ten dollars, he or she shall thereupon be permitted to enter the quantity of land specified.

• • •

Sec. 6. *And be it further enacted*, That no individual shall be permitted to acquire title to more than one quarter section under the provisions of this act.

The Statutes at Large, Treaties and Proclamations of the United States of America from December 5, 1859 to March 3, 1863.

THE RIGHT TO OWN LAND: HENRY GEORGE, JR.'S "THE LANDS OF THE UNITED STATES," FROM *THE LIFE OF HENRY GEORGE*

"Jus' som'thin' that was his. Somethin' he could live on and there couldn't nobody throw him off of it."

Of Mice and Men, 76

An influential critic of land monopolies in the nineteenth century was a newspaperman and economic theorist named Henry George. George moved to California in 1857 and remained for twenty-three years. In 1871 he wrote "Our Land and Land Policy," and in 1879 he incorporated those ideas into a book entitled *Progress and Poverty* in which he set forth his views on land ownership. One situation that had to be remedied, according to George, was the ownership by a few or by big corporations of huge tracts of land at the same time that individual farmers had no way to work their own farms and had to rent land from the land-wealthy.

George's son, Henry George, Jr., summarized his father's land policy in a chapter of his book on Henry, Sr., setting forth the history of land ownership in the United States in general and in California in particular at a time when the buying up of land by industries and the railroads threatened the ideal of farms and homes for all. George's answer was to tax land alone, thus discouraging the accumulation of huge tracts of land in the hands of a very few.

FROM HENRY GEORGE, JR., "THE LANDS OF THE UNITED
STATES" (1900)

The secret of the confidence of Americans in their own destiny and the reason of their cheerful welcome to the down-trodden of every nation, lay in the knowledge of the "practically inexhaustible" public domain spreading over the great Western country that would provide farms and homes for all. But beginning with the Civil War period, a policy of dissipation of the public lands commenced, and so great have been the various kinds of grants, especially to the railroads, up to 1870, that continuing at the same rate, all the available arable land will be given away by 1890.

• • •

In California, twenty-four times as large as Massachusetts and with but 600,000 inhabitants, free land should be plentiful; yet the notorious fact is that so reckless has been the land policy that the immigrant in 1871, has, as a general thing, to pay a charge to middlemen before he can begin to cultivate the soil. Already individuals hold thousands and hundreds of thousands of acres apiece. Across many of these vast estates a strong horse cannot gallop in a day, and one might travel for miles and miles over fertile ground where no plow has ever struck, but which is all owned, and on which no settler can come to make himself a home, unless he pay such a tribute as the lord of the domain may choose to exact.

Land, that part of the globe's surface habitable by man, is the storehouse from which he must draw the material to which his labour must be applied for the satisfaction of his desires. It is not wealth, since wealth is the product of human labour. It is valuable only as it is scarce. Its value differs from that of, say a keg of nails, for the nails are the result of labour, and when labour is given in return for them the transaction is an exchange; whereas, land is not the result of labour, but the creation of God, and when labour must be given for it, the result is an appropriation.

• • •

Now the right of every human being to himself is the foundation of the right of property. That which a man produces is rightfully his own, to keep, to sell, to give or to bequeath, and upon this sure title alone can ownership of anything rightfully rest. But man has also another right, declared by the fact of his existence—the right to the use of so much of the free gifts of nature as may be necessary to supply all the wants of that existence, and which he may use without interfering with the equal rights of anyone else; and to this he has a title as against all the world.

To permit one man to monopolize the land from which the support of others is to be drawn, is to permit him to appropriate their labour.

• • •

The same causes which have reduced 374,000 land-holders of England in the middle of the last century to 30,000 now are working in this country. Not only are large bodies of new lands being put in the hands of the few, but a policy is pursued causing the absorption of the small farms into large estates.

• • •

When we consider what land is; the relations between it and labour; that to own land upon which a man *must* gain his subsistence is practically to own the man himself, we cannot remain in doubt as to what should be our policy in disposing of our public lands.

They should be given to actual settlers, in small quantities without charge.

But this policy would affect only the land that is left. It would still leave the great belts granted to railroads, the vast estates—the large bodies of land everywhere the subject of speculation. Still would continue the tendency that is concentrating ownership in the older settled States. . . .

Why should *we* not go back to the old system, and charge the expense of government upon our lands?

Land taxation does not bear at all upon production; it adds nothing to prices, and does not affect the cost of living. As it does not add to prices, it costs the people nothing in addition to what it yields the Government; while as land cannot be hid or moved, this tax can be collected with more ease and certainty, and with less expense than any other tax; and the land-owner cannot shift it to any one else.

The Life of Henry George (New York: Doubleday and McClure).

THE BANKHEAD-JONES FARM TENANT ACT

The Bankhead-Jones Farm Tenant Act was passed in 1937 in response to the devastation that the Great Depression of the 1930s had brought down on the small farmers of the country. Drought and decreased fertility caused by lack of proper crop rotation, along with land foreclosures by banks, had displaced hundreds of thousands of farmers, many of whom migrated to California in search of land with readily available water. Most of these people remained landless in California, eking out a marginal existence as migrant farm workers.

This act was designed to alleviate the hardships placed on those with no land to farm—"farm tenants, farm laborers, sharecroppers." The aid was given in the form of bank loans intended to help in the purchase of land for farming.

The point here is that land ownership was found to be a partial solution to the problem of homelessness that had developed in the first half of the twentieth century. Carey McWilliams, an advocate for migrant workers, recommended, as a partial solution to the workers' problems, the possibility of owning their own land through such bills as the Bankhead-Jones Farm Tenant Act:

It is designed to make the "agricultural ladder"—from farm laborer to tenant to farm owner—a present-day reality. The better type of dispossessed tenants or farm owners are carefully selected; if they are burdened with debt, an attempt is made to scale down or otherwise adjust the debts. A fair-sized farm is then selected in the community and the necessary soil tests are made. Through a government loan, the client is placed in possession of the farm and given, in addition, an operating loan for the purchase of necessary equipment, livestock, and seed. . . . In 1939 the FSA [Farm Security Administration] helped more than 200,000 farmers in the organization of small service co-operatives for purchase of machinery, trucks, and livestock. That the individual rehabilitation program has been fairly successful to date is indicated by the fact that the government estimates it will eventually be repaid 85 per cent of the full amount of the loans which have been made. Farm families have been given a respite—a chance to live.[5]

FROM THE BANKHEAD-JONES FARM TENANT ACT (1937)

An Act

To Create the Farmers' Home Corporation, to promote more secure occupancy of farms and farm homes, to correct the economic instability resulting from some present forms of farm tenancy, and for other purposes.

Be it enacted by the Senate and House of Representatives of the United States of America in Congress assembled, That this Act may be cited as "The Bankhead-Jones Farm Tenant Act."

Title I—Farm Tenant Provisions
Power of Secretary

Section 1. (a) The Secretary of Agriculture (hereinafter referred to as the "Secretary") is authorized to make loans in the United States and in the Territories of Alaska and Hawaii and in Puerto Rico to persons eligible to receive the benefits of this title to enable such persons to acquire farms.

(b) Only farm tenants, farm laborers, sharecroppers, and other individuals who obtain, or who recently obtained, the major portion of their income from farming operations shall be eligible to receive the benefits of this title. In making available the benefits of this title, the Secretary shall give preference to persons who are married, or who have dependent families, or, wherever practicable, to persons who are able to make an initial down payment, or who are owners of livestock and farm implements necessary successfully to carry on farming operations. No person shall be eligible who is not a citizen of the United States.

(c) No loan shall be made for the acquisition of any farm unless it is of such size as the Secretary determines to be sufficient to constitute an efficient farm-management unit and to enable a diligent farm family to carry on successful farming of a type which the Secretary deems can be successfully carried on in the locality in which the farm is situated.

• • •

Title II—Rehabilitation Loans
Borrowers and Terms

Sec. 21. (a) Out of the funds made available under section 23, the Secretary shall have power to make loans to eligible individuals for the purchase of livestock, farm equipment, supplies, and for other farm needs (including minor improvements and minor repairs to real property), and for the refinancing of indebtedness, and for family subsistence. . . .

(c) Only farm owners, farm tenants, farm laborers, sharecroppers, and other individuals who obtain, or who recently obtained, the major portion of their income from farming operations, and who cannot obtain credit on reasonable terms from any federally incorporated lending institution, shall be eligible for loans under this section.

• • •

Transactions With Corporations

Sec. 46. Nothing in this Act shall be construed to authorize the making of any loan, or the sale or other disposition of real property of any interest therein, to any private corporation, for farming purposes.

The Statutes at Large, Treaties and Proclamations of the United States of America.

A REVERSAL OF THE JEFFERSONIAN IDEAL: CAREY MCWILLIAMS' *ILL FARES THE LAND*

Along with John Steinbeck, Carey McWilliams was considered one of the most dangerous men in California by the farm bureaus because of his interest in seeking equity for farm laborers. McWilliams' most famous book, *Factories in the Fields,* outlining what had caused the end of the small family farm in California and the conditions under which farm laborers struggled, was published in 1939. The following excerpt, from his second volume, *Ill Fares the Land* (1942), shows just how extensive the holdings of some of California's farmers were and how far land ownership had gotten away from the simple family farm described in *The Red Pony.*

FROM CAREY MCWILLIAMS, *ILL FARES THE LAND* (1942)

In the course of investigating a strike which occurred at Marysville, California, in May 1939, in which several hundred dust-bowl migrants were involved, Senator La Follette turned up some interesting facts about one of California's "embattled farmers." Here is what a typical farm factory looks like. The Earl Fruit Company is an operating company which, in turn, is owned by a holding company, the Di Giorgio Fruit Corporation. Earl Fruit Company operates, under a centralized management and as one unit, 27 farm properties in California, and leases 11 additional properties. It purchases, moreover, a considerable amount of fresh fruit grown by small orchardists. It owns 11 packing houses in California and packs and markets, for other growers, about a thousand cars of fruit each year. A typical modern industrial enterprise, it has reached out to control related lines of business. It owns a 95 per cent stock interest in the Klamath Lumber and Box Company (with a capacity of 25,000,000 feet of lumber a year) so that it does not have to pay a profit on the boxes and crates used in packing fruit. It controls two wineries in California, one of which is the largest in the United States. The parent company, moreover, owns a 37 ½ per cent stock interest in the huge Italian Swiss Colony (one of the largest combination vineyards and wineries in California). But Joe Di Giorgio is a fruit merchant as well as a fruit grower. So the Earl Fruit Company owns the Baltimore Fruit Exchange and has important holdings in fruit auction houses in Chicago, New York, Cincinnati, and Pittsburgh. During the last three years, the company has employed an average of

2887 agricultural workers. It is, indeed, a new type of farm that employs 3000 workers throughout the year and has an annual payroll of $2,400,000 for agricultural workers. To provide accommodations for this army of workers, a company town of 350 dwellings has been established with bunkhouse accommodations for 2500 additional employees. Through still another subsidiary, the company owns 13,833 acres of orchard lands in other states. In 1938 the book value of the land and improvements of Di Giorgio Fruit Corporation was $10,955,418.84; and it made annual sales of about seven million dollars. Out of 5000 migrants who find employment in Sutter County, during the peach and pear harvest, over one half are employed by this one corporation. (17, 19)

Boston: Little, Brown.

NOTES

1. Roy H. May, Jr., *The Poor of the Land* (Maryknoll, N.Y.: Orbis Books, 1991), p. 52.
2. John R. Commons, *A History of Labour in the United States* (New York: Macmillan, 1918), pp. 522–535.
3. John Hart, *The Spirit of the Earth* (New York: Paulist Press, 1984), p. 84.
4. John Steinbeck, *The Harvest Gypsies* (Berkeley: Heyday Books, 1988), pp. 58–59.
5. Carey McWilliams, *Factories in the Fields* (Boston: Little, Brown, 1939), pp. 189–210.

TOPICS FOR WRITTEN OR ORAL EXPLORATION

1. Locate at least two people who have owned pieces of land for a number of years and interview them. What do the land and land ownership mean to them? Compare their attitudes with George's. Is there any religious dimension to their reactions to land? Explain.

2. Read the first two chapters of Henry David Thoreau's *Walden.* Does Thoreau appear to have different ideas about land and land ownership than those presented in these excerpts? Explain.

3. Make an argument, using Thoreau's writing and your interviews with landowners, that owning land can be more of a burden and a restriction on freedom than a means of securing freedom.

4. Play the same daydreaming game that George plays and that Thoreau experiences: What would you need minimally to subsist on a piece of land? Explain in detail. Exactly how much money would you need to get started? What would the variables be? How would your calculations differ depending on location? What would you have to give up in your life to do this?

5. What would put Lennie and George at a disadvantage in applying for a loan under the Bankhead-Jones Act? How would the act have to read for them to be treated equitably? Assume you are in the United States Senate. Have a debate on this issue. What would be accomplished by letting the act stand as it is, and what benefit would come from changing it?

6. Construct a detailed argument about the correlation between land ownership and civic responsibility. Use examples from your own observation.

7. Debate this issue: That the future of democracy depends on widespread equitable ownership of land.

8. Contrast the life that Jody lives, especially with regard to his closeness to nature, with the life you lived at that same age. What benefits do you see, if any, in either way of life? What losses?

SUGGESTIONS FOR FURTHER READING

Abernathy, Thomas Perkins. *Western Lands and the American Revolution.* New York: D. Appleton, 1937.

Abrams, Charles. *Revolution in Land.* New York: Harper and Brothers, 1939.

Bertrand, Alvin Lee. *Rural Land Tenure in the United States.* Baton Rouge: Louisiana State University Press, 1961.

Hart, John. *The Spirit of the Earth: A Theology of the Land*. New York: Paulist Press, 1984.

Lilburne, Geoffrey R. *A Sense of Place*. Nashville: Abington Press, 1989.

Livermore, Shaw. *Early American Land Companies*. New York: Commonwealth Fund, 1939.

Robinson, William Wilcox. *Land in California*. Berkeley: University of California Press, 1948.

Rolle, Andrew F. *California: A History*. New York: Thomas Y. Crowell, 1969.

Speek, Peter Alexander. *A Stake in the Land*. New York: Harper Brothers, 1921.

Virtue, George Olion. *British Land Policy and the American Revolution*. Lincoln: University of Nebraska Press, 1953.

Winter, Gibson. *Liberating Creation: Foundations of Religious Social Ethics*. New York: Crossroad, 1981.

4

The Vagrant Farm Worker:
Homeless in Paradise

One of the major characteristics of settlement in California from the early nineteenth century to the present has been the growth of a highly visible group of males uncommitted to families. In the nineteenth century, these were the monks, trackers, guides, mountain men, miners, and cowboys. For many reasons, partly because of the dangerous, rough, and risky nature of the endeavor and partly because many set out planning to return home after they made their fortunes, this was not a domestic society, but a group made up largely of men. For example, it has been estimated that about 25,500 men traveled through South Pass to California from the East in 1849. Only 3,000 women made that trip. This was in keeping with the largely male populations of soldiers, trappers, and scouts that had preceded them. Transience and instability went along with this life.

In the twentieth century we see typically the hobos, migrant ranch hands, and migrant farm workers like George and Lennie and their co-workers. The rootlessness and wandering engendered by the westering tradition in which pioneers led a life of moving ever farther west is found in *The Red Pony* in the character of the old paisano, who had been a migrant worker in his prime and now seeks a place of reference, his birthplace, to which he returns to die. It can also be seen in the grandfather's pioneering past and in Billy Buck's father, who lived the life of a wandering mountain man. In *Of Mice and Men*, all of the characters except Curley and his father are without real homes or land. Most of George and Lennie's associates are like them, constantly on the move from place to place, seemingly looking for something they can never find. There is also in the nineteenth century and in the first decades of the twentieth century—in the lives of the bindle stiffs—a marked absence of one of the characteristics of stability: respectable wives and mothers and family.

The lives of these migrants are unnatural in part because they seem to have no family history, a situation that can be seen in the pioneers who left lives and traditions behind them. In *The Red Pony* Carl Tiflin is disdainful of the meaning of history to the old paisano and to the grandfather. In *Of Mice and Men*, the reader knows only the sketchiest details of Lennie's history. Of George's history the reader knows virtually nothing, and the same is true of most of the other characters. Understandably, George does all he can to keep secret his and Lennie's recent history. Most of the ranch hands just disappear, a situation that explains the amazement of one of the hands who finds a letter to the editor of a magazine written by a former fellow worker. For a brief instant one of the workers has a history.

These large, visible groups of unattached men lived largely outside any domestic family unit. Ranch hands like Billy Buck and his father before him fall into this category. In *Of Mice and Men*, the reader sees a group of both young and old single men who live in a dormitory-style bunkhouse. None of them seems to have a home or family. The women are neither wives nor mothers, but prostitutes. The family parlors are actually the parlors in houses of prostitution.

In *The Red Pony* and *Of Mice and Men* John Steinbeck presents two vastly different kinds of life lived by farm workers in California. The two books represent the two stages of agricultural labor in the Golden State, named in part for the richness of its golden harvests of oranges and wheat. In *The Red Pony* the reader sees the farm laborer in a position typical at the turn of the century—the laborer, Billy Buck is a cowhand who has a home provided for him on a small family ranch or farm in the bunkhouse in which he lives alone, takes his meals with the family, works side by side with the farm owner, and has become a long-standing member of the

The solitary male in the west: a mountain man. From an 1890 photograph.

Men without families: A lodging house interior in old San Francisco. From *Century Magazine*, 1890.

farmer's family, taking as much of a hand as the boy's father in rearing the young Jody. Except in the administration of discipline, Billy even supersedes the Tiflins, acting as Jody's surrogate parent. He stays in one place, having as much investment in the ranch and in the surrounding community, where he is known and respected, as if he were the ranch owner instead of a cowhand. Billy Buck and his kind were soon obsolete, however.

In *Of Mice and Men* we see quite a different agricultural situation, one that quickly supplanted the small family ranch or farm on which a few laborers lived and worked fairly permanently. The size of the typical spread is now so large that it takes a big crew of men instead of just two to do the harvesting. The typical small chicken ranch that Crooks' father once had and the small farm that George and Lennie dream of are things of the past. Now the work on the large farm is mainly seasonal, so that all but three or four of the dozens of workers live on the same farm for only a brief while before moving to the next job at another huge spread, unless, like Candy and Crooks, they are incapable of moving and so are in a suspended state of homelessness on one ranch. No longer does the worker have private quarters in the bunkhouse; except for the African-American stablehand, Crooks, who is segregated because of his race, these men live together like schoolboys, dormitory style, in a bunkhouse. They are called bindle stiffs, bindles being the packs of belongings they carry on their backs as they move from job to job.

There is no true family in *Of Mice and Men* as there is in *The Red Pony*. The relationship between the farm owners and the farm workers is cold and impersonal, governed solely by what the workers can contribute to the profit-making enterprise. When their usefulness is over, they can, like old Candy, expect to be "canned" and thrown out "on the county" (60).

From the turn of the century until World War II, the years comprising the chronological setting of the two Steinbeck stories, the agricultural worker in the United States was in crisis, and nowhere was the crisis more acute than in California. Even from the time of California's settlement, the farm labor situation there was far different from that in other parts of the country, for the small family farm or ranch in California always existed in the shadow of agribusiness and the thousand-acre spread. Wheat became the new "gold" of California in the 1880s, especially in the San Joaquin and Sacramento valleys, and the large-scale agribusinesses that turned to wheat production were more interested in handsome profits than in the welfare of the workers or the well-being of the state.

To secure large profits, agribusinesses not only began to squeeze out the few small farms, but began depending on cheap labor, much of it after the middle of the nineteenth century being Chinese. Then, in 1882, in an attempt to protect the jobs and wages of white Americans, the Chinese Exclusion Act was passed. The new class of laborers, like the Chinese before them, were rootless, landless, and at the bottom of the social scale. Working and living conditions were abominable from the first, with long, hard hours, wages lower than even those of the lowest-paid factory workers, only filthy tents to live in, and only temporary employment doing seasonal work. Before 1900 workers' objections to work conditions were disorganized and confined to one ethnic group or one ranch and addressed only working and living conditions, not loss of basic rights. The lack of any sustained and widespread effective organization could be explained by the fact that workers generally believed that they would soon graduate to permanent jobs, that the transient life would soon be over. Obviously, this is the dream of George and Lennie. Instead, they protested with their feet—just left one intolerable situation for a new job on another farm. So before the twentieth century there was no challenge to employers to improve working conditions, pay better wages, or extend any power to the workers.

Where did these migrant workers come from? Some were small farm owners who had been squeezed out by large agribusinesses, and some were farm hands like Billy Buck who found themselves out of work when small farms folded. The process is explained by Carey McWilliams:

> For these hired hands are scattered about on different farms; they are not all dramatically bunched in one area. The consequences of such a process are seldom enacted before our eyes. Displaced hired hands just vanish, one by one, into an anomalous and shadowy obscurity. The farm laborer, it has been said, "is a voiceless fellow who looks for a job somewhere else if he can't find it on the farm, and not much is heard from him." In the same way, a tenant who has been forced off the land in Iowa, by rising rentals and the con-

solidation of farm units, moves quietly out of the community in an
effort to find a farm somewhere else.[1]

At the turn of the century, a few voices were raised against the
inequity of the situation, but none prevailed. So from the turn of
the century until World War II, the farm workers of California led
a hard existence and frequently protested, without much success,
to change their lot.

In the first decade of the twentieth century, although the miserable conditions of migrant workers began attracting the attention
of national labor movements, few of these organizations, like the
American Federation of Labor, would lend their support to farm
workers. The exception was the Industrial Workers of the World
(IWW), or the ''Wobblies,'' as they were called. The Wobblies were
involved in numerous violent confrontations between farm owners
and workers before World War II, the first of which was the Wheatland hop pickers' protest of 1913, which resulted in the deaths of
four people.

The protest began after a man named Durst, one of the largest
employers of farm labor in California, advertised widely for employees for the season, specifying that he could use 2,700 laborers.
When some 2,800 workers came to his wheat farm looking for
work, Durst hired only 1,500, who, because of the critical shortage
of work, were willing to work for starvation wages. They were
housed in filthy pup tents made of twigs and rags, some of them
open to the sky. Among those put to work were 250 children. Only
eight small toilets were provided for over 1,800 workers. As a result a number of the workers and their children immediately got
ill. The only water available was miles away from their living quarters and the fields in which they worked, and their only drink was
lemonade made of citric acid which Durst's brother sold to them
for a nickel a glass. Their only source of food was a company-
owned commissary that sold groceries to them at highly inflated
prices. And their wages, much lower than those Durst had advertised, ranged from seventy-five cents to one dollar a day. It was
Durst's hope that the low wages and intolerable conditions would
prompt some of them to leave before he had paid them the full
amount for the labor they had done. Coached by the IWW, the
newly hired workers demanded decent housing and food and bet-

ter wages. When Durst refused to meet their demands, they, in turn, refused to work, assembling peacefully to sing union songs.

Claiming inaccurately that a mob of violent men had taken over his farm, Durst summoned law enforcement officers, who came ready to arrest the ringleaders and disperse the workers, firing a shot into the crowd to terrorize them into submission. Instead of silencing and subduing the group, however, the shot enraged the workers. They began attacking the officers, who in turn continued to fire into the crowd. Two people on either side of the fray were shot; the law officers returned to get help from the National Guard, while the workers immediately left the area. One positive result was the creation of the Federal Commission of Immigration and Housing to address the welfare of migrant workers. From this moment on the leaders of the Wobblies were hunted down and arrested. Nevertheless, Wobbly activism and membership increased. In 1915 the state of California intensified its crackdown on the Wobblies, and by 1917 the federal government had joined its power to the cause.

From 1917 to 1920 the farm employers, who found themselves with a labor shortage, wanted not just labor but very cheap labor. Obliging schools in districts with large farms released children for weeks during harvest time to work in the fields. They were paid per month in dollars equivalent to their years in age. So a ten-year-old would be paid ten dollars a month. Young women were also recruited as migrant workers. They were paid twenty-five cents an hour, out of which they paid their room and board.

Writing of the years of the bindle stiffs like Lennie and George, Carey McWilliams points out the inequities in the California agricultural system:

> By the end of the war, a kind of industrial feudalism had been established in California agriculture, with the great lords of the land more firmly in control than they had ever been and more conscious of their power. The bases for this power, in the main, consisted of two factors: the type of ownership involved and the existence of an army—a vast army augmented during the period by Chinese, ex-prostitutes, deaf mutes, orphaned children, women and conscripted labor—by the utilization of which great profits were made. The profits went, of course, to the same small clique to which they had always gone.[2]

In the wake of Wheatland and other labor unrest, large organizations of farmers grew up that were hostile to farm laborers in conflict with owners. Owners used these groups to argue that labor reforms being introduced in industry, such as workers' compensation, should not apply to farm labor. The efforts of the Farmers' Protection League, for instance, resulted in the sound defeat of the eight-hour day proposal in 1914.

In the 1920s, which saw rapid growth in impersonal, commercial farming and of farm owners' cooperatives which worked to the detriment of the laborers, any mutual interests that farm worker and owner may have shared largely disappeared. The old bindle stiffs, like George and Lennie, were rapidly disappearing from the scene, replaced by homeless *families*, all of whom worked in the fields, many living in their old cars, which gave them the means to move from ranch to ranch. Still, as Carey McWilliams reported in 1940, the bindle stiffs were still wandering from farm to farm:

> Bindle stiffs, bums and hoboes of former years used to plod their way on foot and by freight cars. In fact, the tramps as such, the authentic hobo of California tradition, has never passed out of existence. Stubble-bearded, with his roll of blankets, he can be seen today plodding along the highway trying to thumb a ride.[3]

Cletus E. Daniel analyzed the situation of the bindle stiffs and migrant families in the 1920s as hopeless:

> As the "golden" decade of the 1920s was moving toward its unexpectedly ignominious end, few workers anywhere in America were laboring under conditions as materially unrewarding, as physically arduous, or as psychologically oppressive as were those employed on California's industrialized farms.[4]

By 1930 a large majority of farm workers in California were migrants whose lack of year-round jobs made them powerless to live decently from day to day or to improve their lot in the world. Agricultural workers of all sorts were routinely paid no more than fifteen cents an hour for back-breaking temporary work, and attempts to organize to improve their lot were met with job loss, eviction from company housing, and, often, physical violence.

The appalling conditions under which migrant families struggled were chronicled by John Steinbeck in 1936 for the *San Francisco*

News, at a time when he was working on *Of Mice and Men,* which was published the next year. Steinbeck, after traveling for months to inspect and volunteer in areas where migrant workers lived, observed several classes of laborers and their families. The least distressed were those who had just lost their own farms, jobs, or small businesses and had begun traveling around looking for work. A typical newcomer to the migrant life lived with his family in a ten-foot by ten-foot house built of corrugated paper which would collapse with the first rain. The next level of migrant worker, who had been on the road a bit longer, lived with his family in a rotten, ragged tent, swarming with flies, in which the whole family slept on one mattress. The migrant family on the lowest level lived in a house made of willow branches and paper. This family no longer had a bed. They slept on a bit of filthy carpet found in someone's garbage. Infants rarely survived in these families, and both children and adults showed the physical and mental effects of bad nutrition.

Historian Daniel sees the turbulence and violence in the clashes between workers and employers in the Great Depression as a direct result of the repressiveness and inequities stubbornly maintained for so long by the owners of large agribusinesses.

> For California's farm employers, the bitter irony of the 1930s was that the ferocity that attended labor relations in agriculture until the end of World War II was a direct product of their laborious efforts to create a farmworker population whose most enduring and praiseworthy characteristic was its powerlessness.[5]

Lennie and George are what have been classified as non-Depression migrants: "seasonal or casual worker[s] who went from job to job in agriculture, industry, or construction."[6] Nels Anderson further describes migratory laborers:

> In this group may be found from 25 to 30 per cent of all migrants who are able and willing to work. In the language of certain charity agencies these migratory persons would be classed as "worth" workers. Among them are many young unattached persons who have not yet become seasoned hobos, and possibly a few migratory families.[7]

New Deal attempts to stem the ravages of the Depression did not have any great effect on farm workers. An example was the Industrial Recovery Act of 1933, intended to improve the lives of laborers, which specifically excluded farm workers from its provisions. The Wagner Act of 1934 also excluded them. And the Department of Labor openly supported the interests of large farm owners as against laborers, giving in to pressure to withhold from destitute farm workers the benefits of the Federal Emergency Relief Administration.

John N. Webb, who studied migrant workers in the mid-1930s, found that the average length of a job for a migrant farm worker was about two months, and that the average pay for experienced farm workers ranged from thirty to seventy-five cents a day. In 1933 the agricultural migrants made, on average, $110 per year. In 1934 the annual average was $124. Half had been on the road for ten years or more, and 18 percent had been on the road for twenty years or more.

By positioning Lennie and George in comparatively decent living conditions in *Of Mice and Men*, Steinbeck draws the reader's attention not to the physical effects of the migrant life, but to the inevitable psychological effects of homelessness and hopelessness.

Of the documents that follow, the first five, from the nineteenth century, depict a migrant, homeless, and family-less way of life in the pursuit of Eden or Paradise: groups of men, largely without families or homes, condemned to lives of constant roving, devoid of stability and meaning and the fulfillment that comes of human, domestic connections.

James P. Beckwourth, born in 1798, became a famous scout and mountain man in the West. He writes an account of a life constantly on the move. Franklin Langworthy, who joined the 1849 gold rush, and John S. Hittell, a resident of California who moved there in 1849 as well, attest to the nomadic life of many residents as well as the scarcity of women and families in the early days of settlement. The picture is one reinforced by historian Josiah Royce. Mark Twain takes a lighthearted view of the California scene, documenting the unnatural rarity of women and children in the mining camps.

The final three documents describe the life of the homeless, single migrant in the twentieth century. The first is from a major government report on migratory labor in American agriculture. Though it was published in 1950, it still stands as an excellent definition of the migrant farm worker and an introduction to the conditions that produced migratory workers and the problems they faced. The second twentieth-century document is from the working diary of a migrant worker. The third is an analysis of the hobo by a sociologist who lived and worked among them.

HOMELESS IN EDEN: JAMES P. BECKWOURTH, MOUNTAIN MAN AND SCOUT

"Why, I'm half horse myself, you see," he said.
"My ma died when I was born, and being my old man was a government packer in the mountains, and no cows around most of the time, why he just gave me mostly mare's milk."

The Red Pony, 72

Beckwourth was a famous mountain man, one of those extraordinary individuals who made his living in the West before the arrival of the many groups of pioneers in the 1840s. Born in 1798 of a mixed-race marriage, Beckwourth left his native St. Louis when he was in his teens and, moving further west, constantly roamed through Utah, New Mexico, California, and other points west, making his living as a trapper and trader of furs and as a scout for the military. His dealings with Native Americans were skillful and sympathetic, if not always wise. (He was not above selling and giving them great quantities of liquor.) For a time he became a member of a Crow tribe and eventually was chosen as their chief. Beckwourth's life of constant movement was typical of the western man of the time. Beckwourth and other scouts and mountain men, soldiers out west, miners, and cowboys constituted a sizeable number of men in the nineteenth century and the first three decades of the twentieth century who were homeless and constantly on the move. They were forerunners in the character of their personal lives to the men in Steinbeck's *Of Mice and Men* who wander from ranch to farm, working for a short while and then moving on.

FROM JAMES P. BECKWOURTH, *THE LIFE AND ADVENTURES OF JAMES P. BECKWOURTH*. WRITTEN FROM HIS OWN DICTATION BY T. D. BONNER (1856)

I staid but five days in St. Louis, which time I devoted to a hasty visit among my friends. I entered into service with Messrs. Sublet and Vasques to return to the mountains and trade with any tribes I might find on the head-waters of the Platte and Arkansas rivers. This country embraces the hunting-grounds of the Cheyennes, the Arrap-a-hos, the Sioux, and the I-a-tans.

All preliminaries being arranged, which are of no interest to the reader,
I bade my friends once more adieu; and, stepping on board a steam-boat
bound up the Missouri, we were soon breasting its broad and turbid
current. We spent the Fourth on board, amid much noise, revelry, and
drunken patriotism. We were landed in safety at Independence, where
we received our wagons, cattle, etc., with which to convey the immense
stock of goods I had brought through the Indian country. We were very
successful in escaping accident in our progress over the plains, until we
reached the ridge which passes between the Arkansas and Platte rivers.
While ascending this ridge, accompanied with Mr. Vasques, I was sun-
struck. (422)

• • •

I forth-with set about establishing sub-posts in various places, with the
Sioux, Arrap-a-hos, I-a-tans, and Cheyennes, and selected the best men
at hand to attend them. I placed one at the mouth of Crow Creek, which
I called my post, but left a man in charge of it, as I was at present fully
occupied in traveling from one post to another. . . .

We had not, as yet, found any customers; but, as we were in the Cheyenne country, I knew some of that nation could not be very far off. I sent
three different messengers in search of them to invite them to trade, but
they all returned without having discovered the whereabouts of the Indians. Tired of these failures, I took a man with me, and started in the
direction of the Laramie mountain. While ascending the mount, I cast my
eyes in the direction of a valley, and discovered buffalo running in small
groups, which was sufficient evidence that they had been chased recently
by Indians. We went no farther, but encamped there, and at nightfall we
saw fires. The next morning a dense smoke hung like a cloud over the
village of the Cheyennes; we ate a hasty meal, and started to pay them a
visit. (426–427)

• • •

While in the midst of my occupations, a messenger was dispatched to me
by the chief of a Cheyenne village, at that time encamped about twenty
miles distant, with an invitation to visit them and trade there. (438)

• • •

"Captain Sublet," I said, "I have promised the Indian that I will go, and
go I must. There has been no trader there for a long time, and they are
a rich prize."

He saw that I was resolved, and, having given me the control of affairs,
he withdrew his objection and said no more.

I accordingly prepared for the journey. Ordering the horses, I packed up my goods, together with twenty gallons of whiskey, and issued forth on the way to *uncertain* destruction, and bearing with me the means of destruction certain. (440)

• • •

Leaving Sublet's, I went down to the South Platte, distant one hundred and fifty miles, and indulged in a short rest, until I heard that the Cheyennes of the Arkansas—those that I first visited—were about to make their spring trade, and I went over to meet them, and bring them to our fort. (450)

• • •

The next morning we resumed our journey to the fort, which we reached after three days' travel. The village had brought a great number of robes, together with some beaver, and a great trade was opened with them. (451)

• • •

As soon as the spring trade was over, I abandoned that post and returned to the Arkansas. Saverine desired me to go and see if I could open a trade with a village of Arrap-a-hos which he had heard was encamped at forty miles distance. I accordingly started in their direction, accompanied by two men. We journeyed on until we had arrived within a short distance of the village, when we discovered on our road a band of three or four hundred traveling Indians. (455–456)

• • •

I had now accumulated a considerable sum of money, and thought I might as well put it to some use for my own profit, as risk my life in the service of others, while they derived the lion's share from my industry. It was now about three years since I had left St. Louis on my present excursion, and I began to weary of the monotony of my life. I was within five days' journey of New Mexico, and I determined upon going to take a look at the northern portion of this unbounded territory. (456–457)

• • •

We shot several buffalo on our way, enough to load all our horses with meat and tallow. We exchanged our effects in Santa Fe for goods, and carried them to St. Fernandez, a distance of sixty miles. Here we established a store as our head-quarters for the Indian trade, where I resided some time, living very fast and happily, according to the manner of the inhabitants. Among other things, I got married to Senorita Louise Sandeville.

In the fall I returned to the Indian country, taking my wife with me. We reached the Arkansas about the first of October, 1842, where I erected a trading-post, and opened a successful business. . . .

When the spring trade was over, I sent all my peltry to Independence, and bought with the proceeds three thousand dollars worth of articles, suitable for the trade in New Mexico. But, on the arrival of the goods, the whole country was in a ferment on account of Colonel Cook's expedition from Texas, which resulted so disastrously for the parties concerned. This affected the minds of the New Mexicans unfavorably for my interest, inasmuch as their former preference for United States novelties was now turned into strong repugnance for every thing American. I therefore could obtain no sale for my goods, and determined to return to my Indian friends. I bought a load of whiskey to trade for horses to pack my goods to California, where I intended removing. I succeeded in my adventure, and obtained forty horses and mules, upon which I packed my merchandize, and quickly found myself on the way to the "golden state."

I started with fifteen men, three of whom were Mexicans. When I reached the Utah country, I found that the Indians were waging exterminating war upon the Mexicans, but I did not learn it in time to save the lives of my three unhappy followers, who, lagging too far in the rear, were set upon by the Indians and slain. In passing through their country I did considerable trading, exchanging my merchandise for elk, deer, and antelope skins, very beautifully dressed.

I arrived in Pueblo de Angeles (California) in January, 1844. There I indulged my new passion for trade, and did a very profitable business for several months. At the breaking out of the revolution in 1845, I took an active part against the mother country, of which I will furnish some details in my next chapter. (464–465)

New York: Harper and Brothers.

HOMELESS IN EDEN: FRANKLIN LANGWORTHY'S *SCENERY OF THE PLAINS, MOUNTAINS AND MINES*

Franklin Langworthy left the Midwest for the gold fields of California in 1850, like most prospective miners leaving his wife behind. After four years he returned to his home in Illinois. His diary includes descriptions of the passage out to the Sacramento area, the scenery and economy of the communities he passed through, his three weeks in San Francisco, and the character of the people he encountered. In both the mining camps and the emerging port city of San Francisco, Langworthy saw what amounted to an overwhelmingly male society. Most of the miners and the businessmen who followed them were either young single men, men who had left their families for good, or men, like himself, who planned to make their fortunes and either return home to their families or bring them out to California after they got on their feet. Many of them moved from camp to camp, following better mining prospects. To the volume of miners and entrepreneurs in San Francisco were added large numbers of sailors putting into port, a significant number of whom deserted their ships. In the city most of the men lived in dormitory-style boarding houses or houses made from canvas. In the mining camps they lived in equally flimsy and uncomfortable quarters, which he describes. Most men were on their own, forming only the most temporary friendships. As Langworthy explains, this situation, without stability and responsibility, created an atmosphere both demoralizing and immoral. In place of a wife and home, these men frequented prostitutes who worked along with the gambling houses in San Francisco and officiated over the shedlike taverns in the mining camps.

The roving life, the male bunkhouse, the weekend trips to brothels, the lack of any permanent ties, which in large measure contributed to the heartlessness and insensitivity with which the men regarded one another—all are reflected in *Of Mice and Men*. George tells Slim, "After a long time [the ranch hands] get mean. They get wantin' to fight all the time" (41). In a perverse search for some human links, the men on Curley's ranch, like the miners, cowboys, and sailors of old California, seek out prostitutes.

FROM FRANKLIN LANGWORTHY, *SCENERY OF THE PLAINS,
MOUNTAINS AND MINES: OR A DIARY KEPT UPON THE
OVERLAND ROUTE TO CALIFORNIA, BY WAY OF THE GREAT SALT
LAKE . . . IN THE YEARS 1850, '51, '52 AND '53* (1855)

The whole region around here is full of little towns that have started into
existence within a few months. Some of these places contain thousands
of men, and perhaps a dozen women. Cooking seems to be one of the
most lucrative employments, and in this business an active woman can
earn two hundred dollars per month. The principal part of the cooking,
however, as well as washing, is performed by men. Fifty cents is here the
price for washing a shirt. A new one costs but one dollar. Miners
therefore find it the best economy to wear a shirt three or four weeks,
then throw it away and buy a new one. The country is strewn with shirts,
many of which are whole but stiffened with dirt. The houses in the towns
are sometimes constructed with logs, but generally are a kind of frame,
the posts set in the ground and covered with split boards or long shin-
gles. The earth is commonly the only floor. Cloth tents are the principal
abodes of miners, and with these airy habitations, the suburbs of all mining towns are crowded. Great numbers are destitute of tents, and sleep
in the open air, or beneath the branches of the trees. In this mild climate,
where no dew ever falls, sleeping in the open air is by no means detri-
mental to health. (153)

• • •

Morality in California is at the lowest possible standard, though a few
respectable persons may be found. In no part of the world does vice of
every species stalk abroad with so unblushing a front. Thieves, robbers,
and gamblers infest every place, so that no man who has money is safe,
unless he keeps constantly on his guard. Your pockets will be rifled in
open daylight, while walking the street, or standing in a store. If the thief
should chance to be detected and brought to trial, if he has gold in
plenty, he generally escapes justice through bribery, or some quibble of
the law. The civil authority seems to be powerless in defending the property or lives of honest citizens. Murders are so common that they scarce
elicit a passing remark, being of daily occurrence. This fearful state of
society we might naturally expect to find in a country situated like this,
where gold is the only object of pursuit, and where there is scarcely any
fixed population at all. All are on the move, changing and shifting from
one location to another. Nothing seems to be thought of or mentioned,
except some scheme to make money. No conversation upon any moral
or intellectual subject is broached. The whole community, high and low,

learned and unlearned, rich and poor, are engaged in one perfect scramble for gold. This one motive absorbs and swallows up every and all other considerations. There are but few here who intend to make this country their permanent residence, hence they feel no interest in its moral and intellectual progress.—Packs of cards are kept in nearly every house, tent, and cabin, and are generally in use either for amusement or gambling. Checkers and chess are seldom played, these games requiring the player to exercise some little thought and reflection. Mental labor of every kind is altogether avoided, and looked upon with contempt by the great mass of Californians. Tippling and profane swearing are all but universal. A residence here at present, is a pilgrimage in a strange land, a banishment from good society, a living death, and a punishment of the worst kind, and the time spent here ought to be considered as a blank period in existence, and accordingly struck from the record of one's days. (191–192)

Ogdensburgh, N.Y.: J. C. Sprague.

HOMELESS IN EDEN: JOHN S. HITTELL'S *THE RESOURCES OF CALIFORNIA*

"[T]hey just come in and get their bunk and work a month, and then they quit and go out alone. Never seem to give a damn about nobody."

Of Mice and Men, 39

John Hittell moved to California in 1849 and decided to settle there. Although in 1868 he writes to interest pioneers and capitalists to move to the state and invest in it, he notes that serious social problems have been created by a population which is largely male and homeless, and that the failure of the government to determine and certify land ownership throughout the state has made the problem worse.

Hittell's argument is especially pertinent to *Of Mice and Men* in that it makes the connection between an individual's character, the stability of a society, and land ownership.

FROM JOHN S. HITTELL, *THE RESOURCES OF CALIFORNIA* (1868)

In the moral and social, as well as in the physical world, cause and effect are inseparably connected; adequate means never fail in leading to correspondent ends; prosperity or ruin comes not by mere chance, but is the necessary result of the adoption of good or evil counsel. The ill-regulated society and unsound condition of business in our state, are traceable mainly to the insecure tenure of our lands; and as a necessary means to attain social, commercial, and individual health, we must have perfect land-titles. I shall speak first of the mineral counties.

It is a necessary consequence of the want of secure land titles in the mining districts, that the inhabitants should be unsettled. There is nothing to fix them in any one place, while many motives impel them to frequent removals; and the result is, that a considerable portion of the mining population is truly nomadic in character. Most of them have poor claims, or none at all; and they enact laws, or establish customs having the force of laws, that all claims shall be small, usually not more than one hundred feet square. These small claims are worked out in a month or two, or at most in a year or two, and then the miner must go. Perhaps he will find his next claim within ten miles, perhaps not within fifty. When he gets a claim he may not be able to work it out; he must not only occupy his claim, but he must work it. If he absent himself from it more than three days, during the season in which it can be worked, for other cause than sickness, it becomes forfeit to whomsoever will seize it. In no case can he who mines in the river-beds, banks, flats, or gulches consider his claim a home for life; in one case out of a thousand it may employ him for ten years. Quartz and tunnel claims are more lasting, and many of them will not be exhausted in a lifetime; but the miners employed in these are a small portion of the total number.

The miner is not only not tied to his claim by ownership, or the hope of long employment and lasting profit, but he is constantly tempted by other tracts which are open to him without price. He may consider himself owner of all the unoccupied land in the country. He can take and use any of it. No one has a better title than he. Every unoccupied gully, flat, hill-side, river-bar, river-bank, and quartz-vein is persistently trying to seduce him. He can scarcely take a pleasure-walk on a Sunday morning without seeing some place which invites him to come there and settle, to desert his old home and make a new one. And when there is nothing to protect him against such temptations, save his belief in the superior mineral wealth of his first location, that belief may often be changed by a very brief examination of the new place. He has no title to the spot where he dwells, no substantial improvements, no property of any kind save such as he can carry on his back at one load.

The world never saw such a people of travellers as the Californians. There are now about 350,000 white inhabitants in the state, and more than 250,000 others have gone "home" during the last twelve years, four-fifths of them never to return. Not one-fifth—probably not one-tenth—of the miners of 1849 are now in the state, and it would be difficult, and perhaps an impossible task, to find a Californian mining town, one-twentieth of whose population has been permanent there since 1850. In regard to the men leaving California, it must in fairness be stated that many of them are actuated by a desire to be with their families, and they see that it is much cheaper for them to go to New York than to have their families come to San Francisco; and there are cases where the families would make very great objection, even overlooking the cost of passage, against moving to a land so far from all their relatives. But, on the other hand, it must be considered also that all the men who leave the state, do so seeing and acknowledging, before they go, that in climate, mineral resources, the profits of labor and trade, the enterprise, intelligence, and generosity of the people, the independent spirit of the poor, the democratic spirit of the rich, and the frank friendliness of all, California is far superior to any other part of the American Union, while it has many advantages in other respects. Such an acknowledgment, coming from men leaving a state with which many of the most interesting associations of their lives are connected, implies a great evil somewhere. Although some of them go "home" because they cannot bring their families to California, yet this is not the fact in one-fourth of the cases; they go because they do not wish to live here, because they will not live here.

Another evil effect of the want of secure land-titles, and the consequent unsettled character of the population, is the want of good houses and substantial improvements of all kinds. The dwellings throughout the mines are, as a class, mere hovels, even in the oldest and most thickly-settled districts. In the towns it is necessary to have some substantial stores, as a protection to the valuable goods kept in them; but with these exceptions, and a few fine residences, even nominal "cities" are collections of shanties, scattered about with little regard to order, and fitted up with little provision for comfort.

The wandering character of the population, and the want of permanent and comfortable homes, render the mines an unsuitable place of residence for families. There are a few women in the mines, and of these few a considerable share are neither maids, wives, nor widows. The general proportion of adult men to adult women, throughout the mining districts, is probably not less than three to one, and to married women, four to one.

It sometimes happens that miners having wives in the eastern states have them come to live in the mines; but in a considerable proportion of cases this arrangement is not a permanent one. Anxious as the inexperienced wife may have been to live with her husband, and willing as she might be to share his privations, the result has often been that she found life in the mines unsuited for herself and her children. There are many good, virtuous, and intelligent women living in the mines, and perhaps as well contented there as they would be in any other part of the world; but there are not enough of them.

If there were not other evil than this scarcity of women traceable to the present tenure of the mineral lands, that one fact would be enough to settle the question that the mines must be sold. The family is no less essential to the good order of society and the prosperity of the state than it is to the happiness of the individual. A community of American families must have permanent homes; they must own the land in fee-simple; and there cannot be a large community of families in the mining districts of California unless the land there be sold.

The scarcity of women is again the first link in a great chain of evils. Some men in the mining counties would like to marry, but cannot find wives to their choice. They must either travel thousands of miles to get a wife abroad, or take some awkward girl just entering her teens, without education or experience in society, and entirely incompetent to take charge of kitchen or nursery. The scarcity of wives and married women converts many men into tempters, and they must cause much misery. And women, knowing that they are scarce, and therefore in demand, are incited to calculate the chances and profits of fidelity and chastity as compared with infidelity and infamy. Family quarrels often ensue, and the state has a sad notoriety for the frequency of its separations and divorces. A trustworthy gentleman informs me that, during a visit to a mining town in a remote part of the state, about seven years ago, he was informed that there were in the town one hundred and twenty-seven women, forty-nine of whom, though married, were living with men not their husbands. The case is certainly without a parallel, in the state or elsewhere; but the condition of affairs in this respect has changed very much for the better since 1855.

The want of families, and the comparative scarcity of intelligent and good women, deprive the community of many of the most wholesome pleasures and ennobling influences which are found in other states. The man who has no wife or sweetheart to work for is improvident; and, unchecked by such public opinion as can reign only where well-regulated families are numerous and society permanent, he gives himself up to dissipation, feeling confident that none of his neighbors will cut his acquaintance on that account.

As the people are among strangers, and do not expect to remain among them long, reputation loses its value, and public opinion its power; and thus forces of great influence in preserving the good order of society elsewhere have comparatively little influence in the mines.

The scarcity of families and the consequent unstable state of society make servant-girls shy of the country, and the few here demand enormous wages—five and six times greater than in New York. This may at first sight appear to be a fact of little importance, but it has really driven thousands of families from the state, and prevented thousands of others from coming.

These various social evils chafe and foment one another, and the consequence is, that the miners who have come to the state intending only to remain a few years are not likely to change their intention. It is of course the ambition of most men in the country to have homes of their own; to have wives and families, to be with them and to enjoy their society. Since they do not propose to become permanent citizens here, if married, they do not bring their families with them; if unmarried, they do not marry while here. The necessary effect of this state of affairs is, that there is an exceeding anxiety to get away from the country as soon as possible. A feverish excitement prevails through the whole people. Speculation has risen to an unexampled height. The game is, to make a fortune in a few months or to be bankrupt; and there are tens of thousands to play at it.

Men complain that they cannot enjoy life in the mines; that life there is a mere brutal existence; and they become desperate in their anxiety to leave it, to go elsewhere, where ease and comfort, permanent homes and social order prevail; where numerous well-regulated families furnish agreeable company for the married, and where numerous accomplished young ladies furnish not less agreeable company to the unmarried. Most men in California do not live here to enjoy life, but to make money, so that they may enjoy life in some other country. Not that the people are parsimonious from it; but they are puffed up with extravagant expectations, or rather determinations. Unless they can earn very large wages, they will not work at all. The merchant will not be content with a regular business, paying ten times as much profit as he could make with a like capital in the Eastern states; he must go into wild speculations, and risk every thing upon a remote chance of making a sudden fortune. The frequency of insolvencies, particularly in the towns, is inexplicable, at first, to a man who comes here without understanding the peculiar condition of our society; and the same man, going through the mines, will be astonished to see that the much-abused Chinese are the only class who are always industrious. The miner will often do nothing for weeks and months, running up long bills for "boarding," while he waits for rain, or the completion of a ditch, or for something else to turn up. He is too high-minded to accept small pay, and would rather be idle—at the risk of boarding-house keeper and store-keeper. His idleness is frequently called "prospecting;" he travels about hunting for a place to work; and this prospecting may be said to employ nearly a fourth part of the mining population. The consequence is, that a large portion of the miners are always moneyless, or provided with an exceedingly small amount of money. At other times they fall upon rich deposits, and they try to make up in dissipation for past privations. And so the mining population comes to be an improvident one—unsteady, fond of gambling, and other wild amusements. The fact is that there is not in the whole world such another reckless, thriftless, extravagant, improvident population as in the mining districts of California.

Another evil effect of our present system of land tenure in the mining districts, is to be found in the gradual lowering of the general character of the population in the mining counties. Most of the steady, prudent, economical men leave the state with more or less money, while the dissipated, thriftless fellows remain; the latter class increasing in numbers, the former decreasing every year. The only means of fixing and increasing the former class, and giving them the proper influence in our society, is to give them permanent homes; and this policy will at the same time drive away the wrecked specimens of humanity among us, and compel

them to seek homes in the Cimmerian darkness beyond our borders.
(437–443)

• • •

Again, the present system exercises a most prejudicial effect upon the
finances of the state, and bears very unequally upon the citizens. The
farming districts, where the inhabitants own the land, pay heavy land
taxes; whereas mining claims pay no taxes at all. The result is, that the
taxation upon the men in the valleys is about three times as heavy as
upon those in the mountains. The miners generally have no homes, and
no fixed property, and cannot be forced to pay taxes. Most of the mining
counties are deeply in debt, and many are going deeper every year. The
only way to equalize the taxation is to sell the mineral lands, and compel
the miner to pay a tax upon his mine, as well as the farmer on his farm.

The proposed sale of the mineral lands is opposed by two arguments:
first, that it will lead to monopoly; and, secondly, that gold mining in
this state is so precarious, that miners could not afford to have permanent
residences and support families. (445)

• • •

All the great social ills which I have mentioned as prevailing in California,
are traceable directly to the roving character of the people; render the
population permanent and you necessarily cure the evils. It is admitted
that our mines will not be exhausted, and that the number of miners in
the whole state will not decrease much, if at all, during the next fifty
years. It is entirely safe to predict that Siskiyou, Nevada, Shasta, Placer,
El Dorado, Plumas, Sierra, Tuolumne, and Calaveras, will be mining in
1950. Now if the mining is to be continuous, why should not the miner
be permanent? There is no necessity that he should be a nomad; on the
contrary, his own pecuniary profit and the welfare of society require that
he should have a fixed residence, and not until he gets that, can he be a
valuable citizen.

But it is said the mining population cannot be permanent, because
mining is a "precarious" business. Well, I should like to know what business would not be "precarious," if conducted as mining has been in this
state during the last ten years. Here are one hundred thousand men,
mostly without homes; not staying in any one place more than four
months at a time, on an average; spending one day out of three in prospecting; refusing to work unless they can make big wages; running suc-
cessively to Gold Lake, Gold Bluff, Kern River, Fraser River, Mono Lake,
and Cariboo;—how could any occupation be other than precarious, managed in such a manner? Of course mining can be made precarious, and

these fellows who are always running about are the very ones to make it so. It will not be made more precarious by permanence. If the five thousand miners of El Dorado, and the four thousand miners of Tuolumne, will just stay where they are, instead of changing places with each other three times every year, they will not lose any thing on the score of the precariousness of their business. I venture to assert that gold mining in California, conducted prudently, is not an uncertain business at all. A careful man can, with a certainty, earn more than he could as a farmer on the prairies of Illinois, where farming is one of the least precarious occupations in the world. The permanent citizen can afford to mine prudently; the nomad comes here to make his "pile" in a few years; he has no wife with whom to live joyously, and, as a matter of course, his mode of mining is precarious. (446–447)

• • •

. . . There are certain places in the mines where the claims are mostly in quartz-veins of deep banks, which will require many years to work them out, and there the population is comparatively stable. Of these places, Grass Valley and North San Juan may be taken as examples. The traveler sees at once, on approaching them, that there are more comfortable homes, more families, and more peace and sobriety among the inhabitants, than in the majority of the mining towns. The difference is a very great and important one, and if it can be removed by elevating the other towns to the level of those two, the sooner the better.

The "monopoly" argument was used in Illinois, against the side of the mineral lands there, and prevailed for a time; the consequence was, the population was made up of vagrants, and the dwellings were all shanties, and society was no society at all. Finally the lands were sold, and the result was a great benefit to the people and the mining districts, in every social and industrial respect. (449)

• • •

The great question is not whether we shall produce much gold or little; it is whether we shall have social and industrial order or disorder, which is equivalent to the question of the permanency or vagrancy of the population. I am confident in the belief that the sale of the mineral lands would cause a considerable increase of our gold yield; but no matter how great a decrease might ensue, state policy requires that the sale should be made, in any case. The gold now dug does little benefit to California; it slips through, like water through a sieve; and serves only to attract the vagrants who visit the state merely to despoil it. All money under heaven will not pay for maintaining a system under which three-fourths of the people of a large district are vagrants, that is, rovers, and where six-sevenths are men. . . .

Now let us turn to the manner in which the land-titles in the agricultural districts have been managed. (452, 453)

• • •

It is fourteen years since Americans became the rulers of California, and land-titles are no nearer a settlement than they should have been twelve years ago, if a proper system had been adopted.

• • •

The injury done to the country by the delay in the settlement of the land-titles is, to a considerable extent, irreparable. That delay has caused us to lose, or has prevented our gaining, a population of a million citizens, of the most valuable class. Two hundred thousand men have left our state forever—half of them because they could not get permanent homes here—and they prevented as many more from coming, who would have come if they could have had certain land-titles. Not less than fifty thousand men have left us because of the unsteadiness of business and the lack of employment, caused by want of unquestioned ownership of the soil. Thus I estimate that the delay in settling our land-titles has cost us two hundred and fifty thousand men, representing a total population of one million persons. The golden flood, the grand rush of business, the unexampled prosperity which passed over the state from 1849 to 1853, has passed away forever; it is too late to repair the damage; fifty years of peace and justice cannot place California where she now would have been, had justice and sound policy been adopted twelve years ago.

Thus I have explained the reasons which caused the desertion of California by many of the best men who have ever visited her shore. Fortunately, every thing in California is gradually becoming more stable; titles in the agricultural districts are gradually being settled; and it is now almost established beyond a doubt, that within a few years the federal government must sell a considerable portion of the land in the mining counties, at least those counties not occupied by miners. The mining, the agriculture, the commerce, the population, and the wealth must continue to increase, and her name shall be glorious in the records of industry and on the pages of history. (460–461)

San Francisco: A. Roman and Co.

HOMELESS IN EDEN: JOSIAH ROYCE'S *CALIFORNIA FROM THE CONQUEST IN 1846 TO THE SECOND VIGILANCE COMMITTEE IN SAN FRANCISCO, 1856: A STUDY OF AMERICAN CHARACTER*

"I seen the guys that go around on the ranches alone. . . . After a long time they get mean."

Of Mice and Men, 41

Inspired by his mother, whom he calls a California pioneer of 1849, Josiah Royce, an assistant professor of philosophy at what was then called Harvard College, published in 1886 one of the first histories of California, based on official records and all the first-hand accounts then available. From his research, Royce decides that the forty-niners' homelessness, vagrancy, and lack of family life led to irresponsibility, misery, and crime.

The similar social structure in *Of Mice and Men* contributes not only to the riotous drinking and whoring of the men, but to their failure to grow beyond boyhood, and because they have no lasting connections with one another, to a cold and mean streak. This is especially true in their treatment of Candy, whose beloved old dog is shot and who knows that he will soon be thrown out with no means of supporting himself. It can also be seen in their treatment of Crooks, who is ostracized and used as a whipping boy and who, in turn, has developed a bitter, suspicious attitude toward the rest of the men.

FROM JOSIAH ROYCE, *CALIFORNIA . . . A STUDY OF AMERICAN CHARACTER* (1886)

The miners themselves were the least likely of all men in California to become wealthy. The high wages naturally meant, for the miners, seldom the inducement to save for their families at home, but almost always the temptation to extravagance. (234)

• • •

The new-comers, viewed as a mass, were homeless. They sought wealth and not a social order. (276)

• • •

Plainly the first business of a new placer mining community was not to save itself socially, since only fortune could detain for even a week its roving members, but to get gold in the most peaceful and rapid way possible. Yet this general absolution from arduous social duties could not be considered as continuing indefinitely. The time must come when, if the nature of the place permitted steady work, men must prepare to dwell together in numbers, and for a long period. Then began the genuine social problems. Everybody who came without family, as a fortune-hunter whose social interests were elsewhere, felt a selfish interest here in shirking serious obligations. (278)

• • •

The camp consisted of a perfectly transient group of utterly restless and disconnected men, who had not the slightest notion of staying where they were more than a few weeks. When a countryside was full of such groups, disorder, before many months should pass, was simply inevitable. (300)

• • •

[Royce refers to a journal by a woman named Shirley who is one of only five women in the mining camp.]

"Shirley" now began to live in her own log cabin, which she found already hung with a gaudy chintz. The one hotel of Indian Bar was near her cabin, too near, in fact; for there much drinking, and music, and dancing (by men with men), went on. . . . An oyster and champagne supper, with toasts and songs, began the revel. Shirley heard dancing in the hotel as she fell asleep that night in her cabin; and next morning, when she woke, they were still dancing. (Royce's note: These "balls," attended by men only, because there were only men to attend them, were not uncommon in the mines.) The whole party now kept themselves drunken for three days, growing constantly wilder. . . . At last they all reached the climax: as "Shirley" heard the thing described, they lay about in heaps on the floor of the hotel, howling, barking, and roaring (350–352).

Every one has heard how, in early San Francisco life, the family ties seemed sometimes almost as weak as the families were rare. Divorces were in proportion far too numerous and easy. Some men seemed to prize their wives the less because of the very fact that there were in the country so few wives to prize. Of all this the early papers make frequent complaint, and the early travelers frequent mention, although the facts are also often much exaggerated. The causes, however, of this too general disrespect for the most significant relations of life, my mother seemed to see as rather deepening. In the new land, namely, to speak of the matter first from the side of the women concerned themselves, one's acquaintances could not always be strictly chosen, nor one's conduct absolutely determined by arbitrary rules. One had to adapt one's self to many people, to tolerate, in some people with whom one was thrown, many oddities, and much independence, so long as the essentials of good behavior and good purposes remained. The difficulty, however, for certain well-meaning but foolish among the younger women, who found themselves in the midst of all this new life, was to sacrifice some of the non-essentials of social intercourse, as they knew them, without sacrificing anything either of their own personal dignity, or of their true delicacy of feeling. Many such women failed to solve the problem. Little by little they sacrificed this or that petty prejudice, which dignity would have counseled them to observe; and so erelong they were socially more or less distinctly and disastrously careless, both as to behavior and as to companionship. But such mild degeneration is not an element of strength in the union of a family. Men often prized their wives less because the wives grew thus foolishly light-hearted, and were, on the whole, less to be prized. Nor was there a lack of fault on the other side. If women fell into these unguarded habits, such as the custom of letting men who chanced to be their friends, and chanced to be lucky, give them, with careless California generosity, expensive presents on every occasion when these friends had made some new success in business, and if such "Californian" ways, however innocent in their beginning, led to misunderstandings in the end: still, on the other hand, husbands who found themselves absorbed in business rivalry with a community of irresponsible bachelors, and who accordingly lamented the hostages that they themselves had long since given to fortune, often neglected without reason their families, and so in time lost the affection that they had ceased to deserve. In short, as my mother (who, in the course of a few years, had occasion to hear of or to see a number of these broken California families) judged the too general trouble, it was one that might be said to lie in the lonesomeness of the families of a new land. The family grows best in a garden with its kind. Where family-life does not involve healthy friendships with other families, it is apt to be injured by unhealthy if well-meaning friendships with wanderers. The lonesome man, far away from home, seeking in all innocence of heart the kindly and elevating companionship of some good woman, the good-humored young woman, enjoying in all innocence also the flattery and the exaggerated respect of a community of bachelors, the foolish husband, feeling his wife more or less a burden, in a country where so few of his friends and rivals have such burdens to hamper them; such are too familiar figures of social life in a new land. From their relationships spring the curious unhappinesses that at length come to mar the lives of so many good, easy souls. Add to the picture the figure of the bachelor friend, aforesaid, venturing not only to flatter, but, in his rudely courteous or in his more gently diffident manner, to comfort the neglected wife, with honest words, and with kindly services; and one sees how much in danger, under such circumstances, may be the true interests of all family-life. If one wants a high average of domestic peace and of moral health, he must not look for it too hopefully in the domestic lives of the most among those who ought to prize one another highest, namely, wedded companions, in very new countries. These people may indeed be wise, and find all that you could wish for in the way of true happiness; but too many of them will be seen to be blind to the worth of their privileges, just because these happen, at that place and time, to be so rare. Such then was my mother's general observation. But she saw many cases indeed of people who were sensible enough to know when they were happy, and to live in the best of domestic relations. Such families were, in their place, the salvation of this restless and suffering social order. For about them clustered the hopes for the future of society. In them were reared the better-trained children. In them careless wanderers saw the constant reminders of the old home. To increase their numbers, to quiet their fears, to satisfy their demands, men were willing to make vast sacrifices. It was indeed largely in the hope of seeing erelong many such families flocking to the State, that those men who felt their own interests in the country to be fairly permanent were willing to toil for order in the arduous fashions exemplified by the great vigilance committees. (404–407)

Boston: Houghton Mifflin.

HOMELESS IN EDEN: MARK TWAIN'S "CALIFORNIA: CHARACTER OF THE POPULATION," FROM *ROUGHING IT*

"Ranch with a bunch of guys on it ain't no place for a girl."
Of Mice and Men, 51

Twain went west to Nevada in 1861, where he did some silver mining, and then on to California in 1864, where he continued his career as a journalist. His chapter on miners in *Roughing It* is a romanticized history of what occurred two decades before he arrived on the scene. There is interest in the fact that the forty-niners left their mark on the scene, even though much of the physical history of their lives—the towns with their stores and houses—has been erased. Communities that were bustling back in the 1840s had disappeared entirely twenty years later, as had the people who populated these communities. This and the general transiency of mining life tend to exaggerate the notion of a society of constant change where history is obliterated.

The real theme of the piece is the absence of women and children—families—in mining camps. The resultant society is abnormal and demoralizing to the men.

FROM MARK TWAIN, "CALIFORNIA: CHARACTER OF THE
POPULATION" (1892)

It was in this Sacramento Valley, just referred to, that a deal of the most lucrative of the early gold mining was done, and you may still see, in places, its grassy slopes and levels torn and guttered and disfigured by the avaricious spoilers of fifteen and twenty years ago. You may see such disfigurements far and wide over California—and in some such places, where only meadows and forests are visible—you will find it hard to believe that there stood at one time a fiercely flourishing little city, of two thousand or three thousand souls, with its newspaper, fire company, brass band, volunteer militia, bank, hotels, noisy Fourth of July processions and speeches, gambling halls crammed with tobacco smoke, profanity and rough bearded men of all nations and colors, with tables heaped with gold dust sufficient for the revenues of a German principality—streets crowded and rife with business—town lots worth four hundred dollars a front foot—labor, laughter, music, dancing, swearing, fighting, shooting, stabbing—a bloody inquest and a man for breakfast every morning—*everything* that delights and adorns existence—all the appointments and appurtenances of a thriving and prosperous and promising young city—and *now* nothing is left of it all but a lifeless, homeless solitude. The men are gone, the houses have vanished, even the *name* of the place is forgotten. In no other land, in modern times, have towns so absolutely died and disappeared, as in the old mining regions of California.

It was a driving, vigorous, restless population in those days. It was a *curious* population. It was the only population of the kind that the world has ever seen gathered together, and it is not likely that the world will ever see its like again. For, observe, it was an assemblage of two hundred thousand *young* men—not simpering, dainty kid-gloved weaklings, but stalwart, muscular, dauntless young braves, brimful of push and energy, and royally endowed with every attribute that goes to make up a peerless and magnificent manhood—the very pick and choice of the world's glorious ones. No women, no children, no gray and stooping veterans—none but erect, bright-eyed, quick-moving, strong-handed young giants—the strangest population, the finest population, the most gallant host that ever trooped down the startled solitudes of an unpeopled land. And where are they now? Scattered to the ends of the earth—or prematurely aged and decrepit—or shot or stabbed in street affrays—or dead of disappointed hopes and broken hearts—all gone, or nearly all—victims devoted upon the altar of the golden calf—the noblest holocaust that ever wafted its sacrificial incense heavenward. It is pitiful to think upon.

It was a splendid population—for all the slow, sleepy, sluggish-brained sloths stayed at home—you never find that sort of people among pioneers—you cannot build pioneers out of that sort of material. It was that population that gave to California a name for getting up astounding enterprises and rushing them through with a magnificent dash and daring and a recklessness of cost or consequences, which she bears unto this day—and when she projects a new surprise, the grave world smiles as usual and says, "Well, that is California all over."

But they were rough in those times! They fairly reveled in gold, whisky, fights, and fandangos, and were unspeakably happy. The honest miner raked from a hundred to a thousand dollars out of his claim a day, and what with the gambling dens and other entertainments, he hadn't a cent the next morning, if he had any sort of luck. They cooked their own bacon and beans, sewed on their own buttons, washed their own shirts—blue woolen ones; and if a man wanted a fight on his hands without any annoying delay, all he had to do was to appear in public in a white shirt or a stovepipe hat, and he would be accommodated. For those people hated aristocrats. They had a particular and malignant animosity toward what they called a "biled shirt." It was a wild, free, disorderly, grotesque society! *Men*—only swarming hosts of stalwart *men*—nothing juvenile, nothing feminine visible anywhere!

In those days miners would flock in crowds to catch a glimpse of that rare and blessed spectacle, a woman! Old inhabitants tell how, in a certain camp, the news went abroad early in the morning that a woman was come! They had seen a calico dress hanging out of a wagon down at the camping ground—sign of emigrants from over the great plains. Everybody went down there, and a shout went up when an actual bona fide dress was discovered fluttering in the wind! The male emigrant was visible. The miners said:

"Fetch her out!"

He said: "It is my wife, gentlemen—she is sick—we have been robbed of money, provisions, everything, by the Indians—we want to rest."

"Fetch her out! We've got to see her!"

"But gentlemen, the poor thing, she—"

"FETCH HER OUT!"

He "fetched her out," and they swung their hats and sent up three rousing cheers and a tiger; and they crowded around and gazed at her, and touched her dress, and listened to her voice with the look of men who listened to a *memory* rather than a present reality—and then they collected twenty-five hundred dollars in gold and gave it to the man, and swung their hats again and gave three more cheers, and went home satisfied.

Once I dined in San Francisco with the family of a pioneer, and talked with his daughter, a young lady whose first experience in San Francisco was an adventure, though she herself did not remember it, as she was only two or three years old at the time. Her father said that, after landing from the ship, they were walking up the street, a servant leading the party with the little girl in her arms. And presently a huge miner, bearded, belted, spurred, and bristling with deadly weapons—just down from a long campaign in the mountains, evidently—barred the way, stopped the servant, and stood gazing, with a face all alive with gratification and astonishment. Then he said, reverently:

"Well, if it ain't a child!" And then he snatched a little leather sack out of his pocket and said to the servant:

"There's a hundred and fifty dollars in dust, there, and I'll give it to you to let me kiss the child!"

That anecdote is *true.*

But see how things change. Sitting at that dinner table, listening to that anecdote, if I had offered double the money for the privilege of kissing the same child, I would have been refused. Seventeen added years have far more than doubled the price.

And while upon this subject I will remark that once in Star City, in the Humboldt Mountains, I took my place in a sort of long, post-office single file of miners, to patiently await my chance to peep through a crack in the cabin and get a sight of the splendid new sensation—a genuine, live Woman! And at the end of half an hour my turn came, and I put my eye to the crack, and there she was, with one arm akimbo, and tossing flap-jacks in a frying pan with the other. And she was one hundred and sixty-five[1] years old, and hadn't a tooth in her head.

1. Being in a calmer mood, now, I voluntarily knock off a hundred from that.

Roughing It. (New York: Penguin).

HOMELESS IN PARADISE: MIGRATORY LABOR IN AMERICAN AGRICULTURE

The problems of the migrant worker in America, having been addressed sporadically by various governmental groups since the mid-1930s, again came to the attention of the executive branch of the federal government in 1950. In this year President Harry S. Truman created a Commission on Migratory Labor to study the character and causes of migrant labor in America and to recommend remedies for the problem. The basic changes recommended were (1) improvement in job rights and employee-employer relations, (2) more stability and efficiency in an attempt to provide workers with continuous employment, (3) improved housing, and (4) a minimum wage.

FROM *MIGRATORY LABOR IN AMERICAN AGRICULTURE: REPORT OF THE PRESIDENT'S COMMISSION ON MIGRATORY LABOR* (1951)

A migratory farm laborer is a worker whose principal income is earned from temporary farm employment and who in the course of his year's work moves one or more times, often through several States. We do not regard as a migratory worker one who is employed at temporary jobs within daily driving distance of his home, nor one who moves his household from one place to another and thereafter remains more or less permanently. In either of these cases employment could be the same as that performed by migratory workers. Whether a person is a migratory worker depends not primarily on the kind of work he does but rather on whether he maintains a stable home the year round. Season[al] and temporary farm work is done by both migratory and nonmigratory workers. As we shall see later, more nonmigratory than migratory workers are employed at seasonal and temporary farm work.

We do not find that people become migrants primarily because they like to be migrants. Nor do we find that any large portion of American agricultural employment necessarily requires migrant workers. The economy of this Nation has a great deal of seasonal employment other than that in farming. Yet it is only in agriculture that migratory labor has become a problem of such proportions and complexity as to call for repeated investigations by public bodies.

Among the reasons for migrancy, the foremost is that many people find it impossible to make a living in a single location and hence have had to become migratory. Technological displacement, business recession and consequent unemployment in industry, drought and crop failure, radical changes in the sharecropper system, lack of education and vocational training—these are among the basic factors responsible for migrancy. The migratory workers themselves, and their employers as well, testified at our hearings that migrants want steady jobs and that, given the opportunity to settle down, they do so. It is true that, for some, repeated moving has become a habit. There are undoubtedly many who, in trying to make a living at unreliable jobs, have become unreliable people. On the other hand, many who are considered by some to be unreliable are praised by others as good workers.

• • •

No large group of migrants has remained permanently migratory. This probably is the best evidence that people are not migrants by choice. . . . Perhaps the "bindle stiff" and the "hobo" of the 1910's and 1920's were the nearest approach to professional migrants this country has ever had. But they, too, have settled down and no longer count significantly in our migratory work force.

In the thirties the largest element in our migratory labor group was the "Okie," the collective name applied to displaced people of the farms and service trades of the "dust bowl" area including Oklahoma, Arkansas, Missouri, and Texas. Many of these people were migratory workers through the thirties but they resettled whenever the opportunity appeared.

• • •

Within the past decade there is much evidence that, with the opportunity to do so, the migrants of today, like their predecessors, drop out of migratory life.

• • •

Migrants are children of misfortune. They are the rejects of those sectors of agriculture and of other industries undergoing change. We depend on misfortune to build up our force of migratory workers and when the supply is low because there is not enough misfortune at home, we rely on misfortune abroad to replenish the supply.

Migratory Farm Laborers and the Community

Migratory farm laborers move restlessly over the face of the land, but they neither belong to the land nor does the land belong to them. They pass through community after community, but they neither claim the community as home nor does the community claim them. Under the law, the domestic migrants are citizens of the United States, but they are scarcely more a part of the land of their birth than the alien migrants working beside them.

The migratory workers engage in a common occupation, but their cohesion is scarcely greater than that of pebbles on the seashore. Each harvest collects and regroups them. They live under a common condition, but create no techniques for meeting common problems. The public acknowledges the existence of migrants, yet declines to accept them as full members of the community. As crops ripen, farmers anxiously await their coming; as the harvest closes, the community, with equal anxiety, awaits their going.

• • •

The evil that the Industrial Commission perceived has grown. In the past 50 years there has been much social progress for virtually all Americans, but for migratory workers depressed conditions still prevail.

Migrants generally are easily identified as outsiders. Their faces are those of strangers and, for many of them, differences of color and other physical characteristics serve as badges of identification. Their heavily laden cars or trucks, packed with beds, cooking utensils, and furniture are easily distinguished from those of campers on vacation. Even their work clothes, by material, style, or cut seem to indicate an outside origin. All along the way are those who take advantage of the migratory worker's helplessness. Professional gamblers, prostitutes, and peddlers of dope follow the work routes to obtain, each in his own way, a share of the migrant's money.

Residents tend to separate migrants from themselves in domicile and law, in thought and feeling. They assign special places to migrants seeking shelter, or leave them to go where their poverty and condition force them. Here they encamp in tents or simply under canvas supported by a rope strung between trees or from the side of the car to the ground. They sleep on pallets, or on bedsprings or folding cots which some of them carry. Where rains are frequent during work season they find shelter in crude shacks. On farms they use what shelter their employers may provide.

• • •

Customs, codes, and laws, like plants, take root, grow, and endure best in soils that stay in place. The customs of migratory farm laborers rarely find their way into codes and laws; at the close of the season when the people scatter, their ways vanish with them.

Established residence is the primary qualification for exercising the right to vote. By the very nature of their occupation, migratory workers find it difficult to qualify. In some States an additional obstacle is the poll tax. It is not surprising under these circumstances that the interests of migrants are easily slighted in the laws.

Take, for example, the laws governing education, relief, health, and other social benefits. Migrants work in communities where they do not live. Since it is not working in a community but living in it that confers a legal right to such benefits, the migratory worker is usually excluded. During the great distress migration of the 1930's, some State legislatures increased these residence qualifications. The migratory worker was adversely affected by this in two ways: (1) It became more difficult for him to acquire legal residence in the State into which he moved, and (2) the State from which he migrated took steps to bar claims based on former residence. These barriers remain generally on the statute books today.

State barriers are compounded and reenforced by those set up in the county. "Willful absence from the county" for more than six months is one device used to deprive returning migrants of their rights. Administrators find residence requirements a convenient reason for denying basic rights to migrants. Thus State by State, county by county, township by township, nearly every unit of government seeks to evade responsibility for these migratory workers.

Domestic migratory farm workers not only have no protection through collective bargaining but employers as a rule refuse to give to them the guarantees they extend to alien contract workers whom they import. These include guarantees of employment, workmen's compensation, medical care, standards of sanitation, and payment of the cost of transportation.

• • •

Beyond wanting migrants to be available when needed and to be gone when not needed, they are expected to work under conditions no longer typical or characteristic of the American standard of life. In a period of rapidly advancing job and employment standards, we expect them to work at employment which, for all practical purposes, has no job standards. In saying this, we refer not alone to such matters as bad housing, poor sanitation, lack of medical facilities. . . . These are conditions which, over the years, have received condemnation, yet despite some improvement, for the most part they remain unsolved problems and there is little organized effort to deal with them.

In speaking of standards and conditions, we emphasize those surrounding the work itself. First among these is wages. To farm labor generally, and to migrants as well, we pay wage rates that are a little over one-third but well below one-half the average wage paid in manufacturing. To be sure, farm workers receive some perquisites, such as housing, which increase their real wages. But when the value of these perquisites for migratory farm workers was investigated by the United States Department of Agriculture in 1945, the average was about 36 cents a day. There is not reason to believe that any substantial change in perquisites has occurred since 1945. Migratory farm workers receive only about 100 days of employment per year; consequently, the average annual value of perquisites would be around $36 and certainly not over $50. By contrast, the perquisites furnished to industrial employees in the form of sickness benefits, pensions, welfare plans, paid vacations, and paid holidays now average approximately $120 per year.

Farm wages as compared with wages of workers in industry have been both better and worse than they are now. Going back to the years of 1910–14, which is the base period for determining parity prices of farm products, farm wages were two-thirds the wages of factory workers. Perquisites for farm workers were greater then, too, because the "hired man" often lived with the farm family. In the depression years, farm wages dropped to one-fourth the level of wages for labor in factories.

• • •

Low wages, well below prevailing standards, are thus a major barrier to farm employment whether for migratory or nonmigratory workers. Next to wages, job security is an important condition of work. While security for most industrial workers is steadily broadening and improving, farm labor generally has only a minimum of job security and migratory labor virtually no security whatever. Comparatively few migrant farm workers return each year to the same farm employer; hence, very few are able to have dependable employment relationships. They do not have the job rights that are conferred through the principle of seniority now widely accepted in industry, or through the protection of Federal and State laws.

For the migrant, there are few elements of stability in his work. What the employer of migratory farm-labor hires is usually not *a man to fill a job*, but rather *labor service* such as picking hundredweights of cotton, hoeing acres of beets, and picking hampers of beans; and the wages are usually piece rates. The employment relationship is highly impersonal. Often the employer maintains no payroll and he does not know the names of his employees nor how many on any given day are working for him. When the work is ready, such matters as experience, prior employment, or residence in the area count for little or nothing. Hiring is on a day-by-day basis. Labor turn-over in a harvest crew may be 100 percent within a week or less.

Washington, D.C.: U.S. Government Printing Office, 1951, pp. 1–30.

LABOR JOURNAL OF A MIGRATORY WORKER

John N. Webb, who studied the migratory worker in the 1930s and wrote three books on their plight, includes in his second volume, *The Migratory-Casual Worker*, the labor journal of a migrant farm worker. Like Lennie and George, this man must move from ranch to ranch to find enough work to keep him alive. Note the frequency with which he must move and the wide variety of work he must do. Also note the very low wages he is forced to accept.

FROM THE JOURNAL OF A WORKING MAN IN JOHN N. WEBB, *THE MIGRATORY-CASUAL WORKER* (1937)

July–October, 1932. Picked figs at Fresno, California and vicinity. Wages 10 cents a box, average 50-pound box. Picked about 15 boxes a day to earn $1.50; about $40 a month.

October–December, 1932. Cut Malaga and Muscat grapes near Fresno. Wages 25 cents an hour. Average 6-hour day, earning $1.50; about $40 a month.

December, 1932. Left for Imperial Valley, California

February, 1933. Picked peas, Imperial Valley. Wages one cent a pound. Average 125 pounds a day. Earned $30 for season. Also worked as wagon man in lettuce field on contract. Contract price, 5 cents a crate repack out of packing houses; not field work. This work paid 60 cents to $1 a day. On account of weather was fortunate to break even at finish of season. Was paying 50 cents a day room and board.

March–April, 1933. Left for Chicago. Stayed a couple of weeks. Returned to California 2 months later.

May, 1933. Odd jobs at lawns, radios, and victrolas at Fresno. Also worked as porter and handy-man.

June, 1933. Returned to picking figs near Fresno. Wages 10 cents a box. Average $1.50 a day, and earned $50 in 2 months.

August, 1933. Cut Thompson's seedless grapes near Fresno for 7 days at 1 ½ cents a tray. Earned $11. Picked cotton one day, 115 pounds; earned $1.

September–November, 1933. Cut Malaga and Muscat grapes near Fresno. Wages, 25 cents an hour. Made $30 for season.

December, 1933. Picked oranges and lemons in Tulare County, California.

January, 1934. Picked oranges for 5 cents per box for small jobs and 25 cents per box for large jobs, Redland, California. Earned $30. Picked lemons at 25 cents an hour.

January, 1934. Went to Brawley, California. Picked peas at 1 cent a pound. Picked 125–140 pounds a day for 15-day season.

February, 1934. Picked grapefruit at 25 cents an hour, Koehler, California. Worked 8 hours a day on three jobs for a total of 22 days. Also hauled fertilizer for 25 cents an hour.

March, 1934. Worked as helper on fertilizer truck at $2 a day for 20 days, Brawley, California.

June, 1934. Worked as circus hand with Al G. Barnes Circus for 4 weeks at $4.60 a week and board, Seattle to Wallace, Idaho.

July, 1934. Tree shaker at 25 cents an hour, averaged $2 a day for 25 days near Fresno.

August–October, 1934. Picked oranges and lemons at 25 cents an hour, working an average of 6 hours a day, for 60 days, near Fresno.

December, 1934. Houseman in hotel, Fresno. Received 50 cents a day and board for 1 month, and 25 cents a day and board for 2 months.

Washington, D.C.: Works Progress Administration.

NELS ANDERSON'S *THE HOBO*

The first and most famous study of homeless men was Nels Anderson's *The Hobo: The Sociology of the Homeless Man* (1923). At the time he wrote the first of many studies of homelessness that would appear throughout the century, Anderson was a graduate student at the University of Chicago. To collect information about his subject, he lived and traveled with homeless men, interviewing them, collecting their songs and traditions, and observing their relationships with each other, their politics, and their sex lives. His academic work began in 1921 with a study of 400 migrants. In the following excerpt, he speaks especially of their solitariness outside the family order.

FROM NELS ANDERSON, *THE HOBO: THE SOCIOLOGY OF THE HOMELESS MAN* (1923)

Why are there tramps and hobos? What are the conditions and motives that make migratory workers, vagrants, homeless men? Attempts to answer these questions have invariably raised other questions even more difficult to answer. Homeless men themselves are not always agreed in regard to the matter. The younger men put the blame upon circumstance and external conditions. The older men, who know life better, are humbler. They are disposed to go to the other extreme and put all the blame on themselves.

• • •

From the records and observations of a great many men the reasons why men leave home seem to fall under several heads: (a) seasonal work and unemployment, (b) industrial inadequacy, (c) defects of personality, (d) crises in the life of the person, (e) racial or national discrimination, and (f) wanderlust.

Seasonal Work and Unemployment

Chief among the economic causes why men leave home are (1) seasonal occupations, (2) local changes in industry, (3) seasonal fluctuations in the demand for labor, and (4) periods of unemployment. . . . The industrial attractions of seasonal work often make a powerful appeal to the foot-loose man and boy. A new railroad that is building, a mining camp just opening up, an oil boom widely advertised, a bumper crop to be harvested in Kansas or the Dakotas fire the imagination and bring thousands of recruits each year into the army of seasonal and migratory workers.

• • •

Tramping is a man's game. Few women are ever found on the road. The inconveniences and hazards of tramping prevent it.

• • •

Tramping is a man's game. Few pre-adolescent boys are tramps. They do not break away permanently until later in their teens. How does the absence of women and children affect the life of the migratory worker? . . . How does the absence of women and children affect the fantasy and the reveries and eventually the behavior of the homeless man?

The majority of homeless men are unmarried. Those who are married are separated, at least temporarily, from their families. Most homeless men in the city are older than the average man on the road and would be expected, therefore, to have had marital experience. They are content to live in town while the younger men are eager to move in the restless search for adventure and new experience.

The Tramp and His Associations With Women

The homeless man has not always been homeless. Like most of us, he was reared in a home and is so far a product of home life. He enters upon the life of the road in his late teens or early twenties. He brings with him, as a rule, the habits and memories gained in the more stable existence in the family and community. Frequently it has been his conflict with, and rebellion against, that more stable existence that set him on the road.

• • •

When the tramp works he usually goes out on some job where there are no women. He may spend six months in a lumber camp and not see a woman during all that time. He may work for a whole summer, along with hundreds like himself, and never meet a woman. Sometimes there are women on such jobs, but they are generally the wives of the bosses and have no interest in the common workers. . . . The only company for such a man is men, and men who are living the same unnatural life as himself.

Chicago: University of Chicago Press, pp. 69–136.

NOTES

1. Carey McWilliams, *Ill Fares the Land* (Boston: Little, Brown, 1942), p. 4.

2. Carey McWilliams, *Factories in the Field* (Boston: Little, Brown, 1939), p. 177.

3. Ibid., p. 307.

4. Cletus E. Daniel, *Bitter Harvest: A History of California Farmworkers, 1870–1941* (Ithaca, N.Y.: Cornell University Press, 1981), p. 103.

5. Ibid., p. 68.

6. Nels Anderson, *Men on the Move* (Chicago: University of Chicago Press, 1940), p. 28.

7. Ibid., p. 29.

TOPICS FOR WRITTEN OR ORAL EXPLORATION

1. Research a recent controversy about attempts to protect American laborers from competition with cheap foreign labor. You might start by querying your own state legislators on the issue. What are the various arguments on both sides of the controversy? Stage a legislative session in which class members argue whether to pass a bill excluding foreign workers from the United States market.

2. Arrange a screening of Edward R. Murrow's 1960 documentary *Harvest of Shame*. Construct questions for a formal discussion after the showing, and carry through on the discussion.

3. Research the indexes of a major newspaper in your area for recent accounts of the actual living conditions of migrant workers somewhere in the United States. Write a paper on what you find.

4. Write your own account, as if for a newspaper, about George and Lennie and their fellow workers, concentrating on the psychological effect of their situation on the spirit. You may use fictional interviews, but try to remain true to the concepts of Steinbeck's work.

5. Write a paper on Cesar Chavez—what his background was, what motivated him, what he worked for.

6. Try to find a copy of the controversial 1970s movie about Joe Hill, a Wobbly leader. After the class has viewed it, film a roundtable discussion of the movie by several members of your community who might have differing views on labor unions and radicals.

7. Try to locate some older people in your family or community who have lived through the thirties and could report on the impact of the dust bowl and economics on their lives.

8. Arrange an artistic performance about the Depression with special emphasis on farm workers, using newspaper accounts mixed with Wobbly and other Depression era songs.

9. From the information you gather about wages and expenses, figure out how long it would have taken a worker in the 1930s to purchase a small plot of land for a subsistence existence. Look at costs in some old newspapers of the 1930s, perhaps in your hometown.

SUGGESTIONS FOR FURTHER READING

Anderson, Nels. *The Hobo: The Sociology of the Homeless Man*. Chicago: University of Chicago Press, 1923.

———. *Men on the Move*. Chicago: University of Chicago Press, 1940.

Cross, William T., and Dorothy E. Cross. *Newcomers and Nomads in California*. Stanford: Stanford University Press, 1937.

Daniel, Cletus E. *Bitter Harvest: A History of California Farmworkers, 1870–1941*. Ithaca, N.Y.: Cornell University Press, 1981.

McWilliams, Carey. *Factories in the Field: The Story of Migratory Farm Labor in California*. Boston: Little, Brown, 1939.

———. *Ill Fares the Land: Migrants and Migratory Labor in the United States*. Boston: Little, Brown, 1942.

Minehan, Thomas. *Boy and Girl Tramps of America*. New York: Farrar and Rinehart, 1934.

Taylor, Paul. *On the Ground in the Thirties*. Salt Lake City: Peregrine Smith Books, 1983.

Webb, John N. *The Migratory-Casual Worker*. Washington, D.C.: Works Progress Administration, 1937.

———. *The Transient Unemployed*. Washington, D.C.: Works Progress Administration, 1935.

5

Losers of the American Dream

Those who sailed from the Old World to the New World, those who joined the American Revolution against the caste system of Britain in order to raise their status in the world, and those who traveled west in pursuit of their very own land were all on a quest for what has come to be called the American Dream. The dream, as old as Benjamin Franklin, with his advice to young men on how to become successful, was still very much alive in the 1920s, by which time it had become transformed to mean a carefree life of plenty and laughter. But from the time of Benjamin Franklin, many were unable to achieve the dream of which they were constantly aware in American society. In the 1930s many had abandoned the aspirations of the pioneers and the American Dream of success, desperately hoping only to survive.

His characters' longing for some version of what we have come to identify as the American Dream, and the dream's elusiveness, are major themes in Steinbeck's *The Red Pony*, *Of Mice and Men*, and *The Pearl*, even though the last is actually set in Mexico. Some of the characters for whom the dream will typically always remain elusive in his novels are the aged, like the grandfather in *The Red Pony* and Candy in *Of Mice and Men*; the physically handicapped, like Candy and Crooks; the mentally handicapped, like Lennie; and those racially discriminated against, like Crooks and the family in

The Pearl. These are the powerless ones and the outcasts who are the losers of the American Dream of success and plenty. Not only do money and success elude them, but most of them struggle with poverty all their lives. Yet for at least a moment, all these characters have dreamed the American Dream.

The grandfather in *The Red Pony* has cherished a pristine version of the American Dream that had little to do with the accumulation of worldly goods and economic power. As a pioneer, he dreamed of following the endless adventure that the unexplored continent afforded rather than pursuing material comfort. His dream might be compared to an astronaut's dream of space travel. But when the grandfather encountered the Pacific Ocean, the dream was over for him.

In a sense, the only way the grandfather can still grasp the American Dream is to relive his adventure by retelling it. Since he is old and the real activity of his mature years is far behind him, and the new Americans like his son-in-law, Carl Tiflin, won't tolerate that repetition, the dream continues to elude him.

Gitano is another old man whose dream has come to be only a decent life in his final days and a decent death. His tradition brings him back to the ranch, where he can only promise to do the simplest chores.

In *Of Mice and Men* the American Dream is understood to be somewhat different. It means independence and self-sufficiency, the freedom that comes from owning land, which in turn means enjoying the fruits of one's own labor. Yet all but the two ranch owners are surely losers of the American Dream. They work hard but are always on the move and on the margins of society. The additional handicaps of a number of these characters make any pursuit of that dream especially futile. Candy and Crooks are doubly handicapped. Candy is old and maimed, having been injured on the job. He can only work at menial chores like swamping out the bunkhouse. As compensation for having lost his right hand while making money for his employers, he has received a bonus of $250 and is able to stay on at the ranch at $50 a month with, presumably, his room and board. His old age, however, means that even this gesture will soon end. He foresees that he will soon be fired because he will be too old to work and that his situation will be hopeless. Economic despair is not the only price Candy pays for his old age. Like the grandfather in *The Red Pony,* he faces

Single men living on the road: bindle stiffs resting from farm work. Photo courtesy of The Bancroft Library.

daily humiliation because of his old age. The ultimate heartache is seeing Carlson drag off his old beloved dog to shoot it.

Crooks is another character with multiple handicaps that keep the American Dream out of reach, for he is isolated and cruelly disparaged by the rest of the men because he is black. One of the first stories Candy tells Lennie and George to introduce them to life on this ranch is to explain how everyone gives Crooks hell when they're unhappy because Crooks is a black man. Candy also tells how one of the workers began fighting Crooks, presumably because he was black. Furthermore, Crooks' race places him in a particularly dangerous position with regard to Curley's wife, whom he knows can threaten him with a false charge of rape, a charge that would lead to hanging, if he doesn't do as she says. Like Candy, Crooks also has the handicap of having been injured in the course of work on the farm.

Finally, there is Lennie, who is doomed in large measure because he is mentally retarded. The initial description of him suggests a mentally retarded man who shuffles, and his speech is childlike. George, who describes Lennie to Slim as "dumb," knows that Lennie cannot be trusted to carry his own work card, and must pry dead mice away from him, repeatedly get him out of town when he gets in trouble, make sure he doesn't say anything to make the new bosses refuse to hire him, and finally shoot him to keep him from being lynched or imprisoned for life.

When Curley's wife finds Candy, Crooks, and Lennie in the stable, she observes accurately, "They left all the weak ones here" (77). In a very real sense, of course, *all* of these characters are weak—far too weak to get even close to pursuing the American Dream, which for them all takes the form of owning their own land.

GETTING OLD IN PARADISE

For the elderly poor—those without family to take care of them—there seemed little hope for a decent old age until the passage in 1935 of the Social Security Act as part of Franklin Roosevelt's New Deal. But for elderly and poor agricultural workers like Candy, there was no relief even then, for agricultural workers were systematically excluded from the benefits of every measure passed to assist the poor. The year 1883, however, saw

A lonely bindle stiff in Napa Valley. Photo courtesy of The Bancroft Library.

the passage of the County Government Act in California, and in 1901 the Indigent Act was passed. This is what Candy is probably referring to when he speaks of being put out on the county. Aid was usually given in the form of food, though sometimes payments of up to $30 a month were made. For those aged who had no place to live, there were county hospitals and almshouses in which the poor who were sick, aged, and mentally defective were all housed together. After 1925, the State Department of Public Welfare began placing sick and healthy old people in separate homes and institutions which were licensed by the state. In 1928 the average amount provided by the state to those who were destitute and old was under $15 a month. Most of those who applied for assistance were old men who had worked in the gold mines, the lumber camps, or the wheat fields of California. In 1930 California passed the Old Age Security Law to help needy citizens. Eligibility was simple and open to migrant farm workers within the state of California as long as they were at least seventy years old, citizens of the United States for fifteen years, residents of California for fifteen years, a resident of the county for one year, and had no children or other person able to take care of them. Aid was limited to a total of one dollar a day. Over the years, the occupation of those who were among the poorest old people, having no other assistance except what they received from the state, was agricultural worker.

In the 1930s several reformers in California saw the pressing need to provide for the elderly poor. One plan, the California Retirement Life Payments Act, was popularly called "Ham 'n Eggs." This was a fairly complicated proposal introduced in 1938 to provide a pension for the aged. Note that Carl Tiflin in *The Red Pony* taunts the old man, Gitano, by saying that if ham and eggs grew on the hills, he could put him out to pasture, like an old horse (49). Carl Tiflin's attitude was very likely typical, because the "Ham 'n Eggs" measure was defeated on the California ballot.

Both Gitano in *The Red Pony* and Candy in *Of Mice and Men* are old men who seek out a small, family-like group in their old age, volunteering to contribute their own limited talents in order to subsist and, in Candy's case, to alleviate his own loneliness and meaninglessness.

Groups working to alleviate the suffering of indigent elderly people in California at the time realized that the answer to many of the physical needs and psychological problems of the aging poor was the establishment of cooperative enterprises. One study made by the state of California in 1937 recommended such groups wherein the poor might find a meaningful and secure existence, where they might continue to work and alleviate the loneliness to which the elderly are susceptible.

The other major class of individuals in Steinbeck's novels who are unable to subsist on their own, much less achieve the American Dream, is represented by Lennie, the mentally retarded companion of George. At the time Steinbeck wrote his novel, mentally deficient individuals were legally defined as "persons in whose case there exists from birth or from an early age mental defectiveness not amounting to imbecility, yet so pronounced that they require care, supervision, and control for their own protection or for the protection of others."[1] At the time the novel is set, the public, influenced by late nineteenth- and early twentieth-century studies of retardation, saw people like Lennie as "useless, incompetent, potentially dangerous and totally parasitic"; even those with mild retardation were seen as incapable of living in ordinary society and in need of institutionalization.[2] Until the middle of the nineteenth century in America, mentally disabled children who needed the support of an institution were only accepted by a few state schools for the blind and the deaf. Under the leadership of Samuel Gridley Howe, the public began to pay attention to the plight of retarded children in the late nineteenth century, and gradually began to establish small schools to meet their special needs. These were eventually replaced by large institutions. Between 1900 and 1920, the idea that all feebleminded people were a burden was replaced by the idea that all of them were dangerous. Despite the need for someone to protect and help people like Lennie, up until the 1920s little was done for mentally retarded adults. When a mentally retarded person reached the age of sixteen, he was excluded from programs and institutions established for those who were then called "the feebleminded." Consequently, in the early decades of the century, retarded men frequently became homeless and were preyed upon by unscrupulous street people. By the 1930s, many mentally deficient citizens, rather than joining society to work after being trained in special schools, remained in such schools throughout their adult lives. Many more retarded adults began staying in institutions during the economic depression of

Living conditions provided for workers on the Durst ranch. A 1912 photo by the California Commission of Immigration and Housing.

the 1930s because it was almost impossible to get them even the most menial jobs. The availability of facilities for adults produced a measure of protection for those who needed it, but it also turned the little schools into big institutions.

Compounding the problems of old age and race discrimination, Candy and Crooks have serious disabilities as results of accidents suffered on the job. Both workers are typical of those injured on the job at farms, factories, railroads, and mines which made millions of dollars for their owners. There was no compensation required by law for any worker who had been injured on the job in the first decades of the century. It was not until 1916 that Congress passed a law providing compensation to federal workers injured on the job; not until 1948 did states adopt workers' compensation laws; and not until 1946 was a federal bureau established to oversee workers' compensation programs to provide benefits for employees who suffered personal injury while on duty. These programs, funded by employers, provided compensation and medical care, death benefits and pensions, and training in new jobs. However, even after 1948 Candy and Crooks would not have received these benefits because the law did not cover most farm workers.

For those like Candy, Crooks, and Lennie who are losers of the American Dream of plenty, there were only two choices: to struggle along alone without the physical or mental capacity for survival or to commit themselves to an institution where they would very likely lose all their freedom and be abused and neglected.

Poorhouses for the aged and institutions for the retarded, the insane, and the disabled were all places where society relegated those whom it didn't want living in the mainstream. Just as Candy fears the county's poorhouse for the aged, George despairs at what will happen to Lennie if "they" "lock him up an' strap him down and put him in a cage," (97) as Slim supposes they will do.

The tragedy of America's dispossessed, however, goes beyond the problem of survival. In a society guided by the American Dream of plenty, those who are incapable of climbing the ladder of economic success have no worth. In this society ruled by the Almighty Dollar, they suffer in spirit. The prevailing system has somehow taken away from them dependable, caring human connections and the independent self-determination of adulthood.

The documents that follow describe the plight of America's dispossessed—those who have lost out on the American Dream. The first selections are from Alice Willard Solenberger's landmark study of homelessness. Nels Anderson, one of the first sociologists to study the problem, makes graphic the hopelessness of homeless, aging migrants, with reference to a particular case; his research also provides further documentation of the numbers of mentally handicapped men who were transients. Carey McWilliams studied migrant laborers at the time John Steinbeck was writing *Grapes of Wrath* and *Of Mice and Men.* His work provides corroboration of agricultural injuries and the campaign on the part of employers to enlist the handicapped in field work. Also included are excerpts from a study by William and Dorothy E. Cross on elderly migrant workers in California who banded together in communities for financial and psychological support. The final document is an interview with an eighty-two-year-old officer in the Salvation Army who has worked with transients and other losers of the American Dream since the 1930s.

LOSERS: *ONE THOUSAND HOMELESS MEN*

Alice Willard Solenberger was one of the first people to do a serious study of homelessness in America. From her position as di-
rector of the Central District of the Chicago Bureau of Charities,
she launched a systematic study of homeless men, the first of its
kind. Although her study was chiefly restricted to homelessness in
the cities, she has much to say about the problems of the aged and
disabled in any part of the country. (She died in December 1910
before she could see her work into print.) The first excerpt is about
the crippled and maimed; the second on the insane, feebleminded,
and epileptic, who comprised a large portion of the homeless population; the third on homeless old men; and the last on how migrant labor in general contributes to homelessness.

Note how strikingly her case study of a feebleminded nineteen-
year-old fits the description of Lennie: childlike, frustrating for his
care-givers, mentally disturbed—even wanting to go someplace
where he could milk cows.

FROM ALICE WILLARD SOLENBERGER, *ONE THOUSAND
HOMELESS MEN* (1910)

The Crippled and Maimed

Two hundred and fifty-four men, or more than a fourth of the one thousand studied, were either temporarily or permanently crippled or
maimed. The disclosure of so large a proportion of handicapped men
will probably provoke questions in the minds of most readers, both as
to whether a similar proportion would be found among other thousands
of the homeless and shifting population, and as to what may have been
the causes and what are the effects of all this crippling of men. It is not
possible to compare the ratio of crippled and maimed in this group with
that of the homeless men at large, because there are no statistics available
in regard to the latter; but . . . there is little question but that the percentage of crippled and maimed is larger among homeless men who have
asked charity than it would be found to be among homeless men in
general; a fact which should be constantly kept in mind lest one fall into
the error of drawing unwarranted general conclusions from statistics
which relate only to a particular, and in this regard a peculiar, group of

men. But whether or not the number of cripples per thousand is smaller among the homeless men in the lodging houses than in this group, the causes of crippling and the ratio in which they appear, and the individual and social results of it, would be much the same wherever homeless men might be studied.

• • •

The Insane, Feeble-minded, and Epileptic

No one who comes in touch with homeless men as a class can long remain unacquainted with the fact that a considerable number of them are mentally defective or diseased. In this particular group of a thousand men, 81 were found to be temporarily or permanently dependent on account of mental unfitness for work. In 52 cases the men were, or had recently been, insane; in 19, feeble-minded; and in 18, epileptic. Four of these were both epileptic and insane, and one was epileptic and feeble-minded. . . . To the number of the feeble-minded might also be added the cases of certain men who, while not actually imbecile, were yet so dull, ignorant, and incapable as to be greatly handicapped by their mental deficiencies.

• • •

The Feeble-Minded

The condition of the feeble-minded man or boy who is found among the homeless is, if possible, even more pitiable and more hopeless than that of most of the insane. For even when he falls into the hands of persons who would gladly try to remove him from the road and provide care for him, in most instances little or nothing can be done in his behalf, for the reason that, after he has passed the age of sixteen, he is not eligible for admission to any institution for the feeble-minded in the United States, except in Massachusetts. The only other institution in which he may be placed for care is the poorhouse, and since in most states he is only *admitted* and not *committed* to this, it is of but little avail to send him there; he will almost invariably wander away and be again upon the road within a short time.

Perhaps no better idea can be given of the problem which is presented to the charity worker when a feeble-minded homeless man applies for aid, than to cite one or two specific cases of this type. A lad of nineteen, who thought he could "weed a garden and water grass," asked us to send him to some place "where little children are" and where he could milk cows. He was taken first to a restaurant, where he ate ravenously, and then to the industrial department of a nearby lodging house, where his ability to work was tested. It was found that he did nothing except when watched, and could not do even the simplest tasks without much explanation and supervision. From a relative, whose address he gave us, we learned that the boy had been for years in the habit of wandering away from his home or from any place where his family put him. They had tried him in public and private schools, and also in an industrial training school, but he could learn nothing and invariably ran away. He had somehow learned how to dispose of things by pawning them and his family found it very difficult to keep him decently clothed, because he would either sell or pawn whatever was given to him. He had once sold a new suit of clothes for 15 cents. His family were utterly discouraged with the problem of his care, and said they would welcome any suggestions or advice. The Bureau of Charities appealed to a child-placing agency for a working home in the country for him, but the lad was too old to be accepted by this society, and, moreover, its agents felt certain that he would run away if sent to a farm. A few symptoms made it seem possible that the boy was insane rather than feeble-minded, and he was sent to the detention hospital for examination, but was dismissed as imbecile, not insane. The effort was then made to send him to the state school for the feeble-minded at Lincoln, Illinois. He was already three years older than the maximum age for admission to that institution, and so a special appeal in his behalf was made to the superintendent of the institution and to the governor of the state. After much work and many delays he was finally admitted to the Lincoln School. Four days later we received word that he had run away, and six months later, dirty, ragged and half-starved, he returned to the Bureau of Charities and begged for food.

Here is another case quite similar. A lad of twenty told us, what was probably true, that he had been taken sick while doing odd jobs at Columbus, Ohio, and that "some one" had put him on a train and given him a ticket to Chicago. Upon his arrival he had been taken by the police from the depot to the county hospital, where he had remained for nine weeks and from which he had just been dismissed. These latter statements were verified. The boy still looked very ill and it was necessary to give him his entire support until he should be strong enough to work. In less than a week, however, he had a relapse and had to be returned to the hospital for several additional weeks of treatment. During this interval his history was looked up, and after much difficulty we learned that his mother had died in a poorhouse in Rochester, New York, and his father in a poorhouse in Jacksonville, Illinois. Also that the boy himself was too feeble-minded to be capable of self-support and had been wandering about the country for some time.

• • •

Among the feeble-minded and epileptic, as among the insane, men occasionally came to the office who had been seriously injured and could not tell just where or how they received their injuries. One of these (who, by the way, had just been dismissed from the House of Correction to which he had been committed for vagrancy), had his right hand so mangled in some sort of accident that the surgeon who examined it said that its use was permanently destroyed. The man, who was of very low mentality, could give few details of the accident.

The feeble-minded are not, as a rule, long-lived. The average age of those who applied to us was much lower than that of the insane. Almost without exception, too, these men were ailing, if not actually ill when they applied.

· · ·

Homeless Old Men

No class of our applicants from among the homeless seemed to be more uniformly hopeless and unhappy than the men who had passed sixty, and who realized that the doors of industrial opportunity were being closed against them and that it was only a question of a short time before they must become wholly dependent upon charity. The tendency of modern industry is to discard from its ranks younger and younger men. If chance throws them out of employment, men who have passed sixty must almost invariably resort to casual labor. It is almost equally difficult for men in their fifties to find well-paid employment, while in certain lines of work men who drop out in their forties or even in their latter thirties are not eligible for re-employment, because they have passed the fixed limits of age which prevail in those occupations. The men of these latter ages who find themselves obliged to apply for charity solely for this reason are, of course, very few in number compared with those who have passed sixty and who find the infirmities of real and not of arbitrarily fixed old age complicating their problems of employment. Many men of sixty, however, are still strong and well, and none of these, if he is self-respecting and under the necessity for self-support, will accept the verdict that he is "too old" to be of further industrial value without a bitter struggle to prove the contrary.

"I am as well able to work as I ever was. Better, too, because I am so much more experienced than a young fellow."

"Experience ought to count for something. I know there is a place for me somewhere if I can only find it."

"It cannot be possible that I am never going to have steady work again. I am not old enough to be thrown out yet. I'll get located soon, but I'll have to ask for a little temporary aid."

Pitifully often have men in the neighborhood of sixty made such statements when applying to the Bureau of Charities for work or for financial aid.

The first time they apply they assure us it will be "only a temporary matter." They are certain that they will soon find work and be able to repay all that may be advanced. Later on in the struggle come confessions of failure and discouragement and suffering. From being usually self-supporting and only occasionally lapsing into temporary dependence they become at best only partly self-supporting with almost continuous need for some charitable assistance.

• • •

"Is tired and discouraged and says he is afraid he will have to give up and go to Dunning [the Almshouse] soon," is an entry on one record.

"Says he is physically well but mentally weary," is another.

"Is having a hard struggle."

"Is as strong as ever, but finds it increasingly hard to get work because he looks old."

• • •

"Has had so little work this winter that he has almost starved but cannot bear the thought of the poorhouse."

"Unable to find any work. Says he is penniless, friendless, and discouraged."

"Has no work yet but says he would rather starve than go to Dunning."

Such entries as these may be found on 50 per cent of the records of the old men applying to the Bureau, and these are not men who have been idle and profligate, but . . . in some cases, business or professional men.

• • •

Most of the [old men] were suffering from diseases or conditions common to old age, such as rheumatism, paralysis, blindness, deafness, etc., from which they were unlikely ever wholly to recover. The "feebleness of age" is the only difficulty entered in the records of 24 men.

• • •

It was old men of an entirely different class who furnished some of our most puzzling problems of treatment. Eighty-five of the 132, as has been said, were of good character and habits, and had always, previous to the advent of old age, been self-respecting and fully self-supporting members of society. With these men the causes which were apparently most responsible for their final dependence were (1) the receipt of irregular and insufficient wages over a period of years which made saving for age difficult, if not impossible . . . (6) ill health or crippling accidents which destroyed earning capacity before sufficient savings for age had been accumulated. . . . I have not attempted to list these causes in the exact order of their importance, for two or more of them so often appeared in a single case that it is difficult to judge their relative values in the whole group. For instance, one man lost all his savings ($15,000) in a bank failure within a month after a fall which broke his hip and made him a cripple for the ten remaining years of his life.

. . .

In a few instances, where men had for a number of years lost all trace of their families, they were able to give slight clues by means of which, with the co-operating help of charity organization societies of other cities, we finally succeeded in finding their friends. But only in some 30 instances altogether did relatives furnish adequate assistance.

. . .

In only twelve cases were we able to secure pledges of enough money from persons interested in their welfare to pay old men small weekly pensions for the remaining weeks of their lives. Those pensioned had all lived useful lives and were dependent in age solely from misfortune. The sums paid to them were $4.00 to $5.00 a week. Some of these men have died, but the pensions of several are still being paid and additional ones for other old men have since been established.

This method of helping is unquestionably the one most acceptable to old men, for it permits them to remain in their accustomed neighborhoods and to be quite independent in their actions. Dread of life in an institution seems to be almost universal among them, although the particular institution most dreaded is, of course, the poorhouse. Unless, however, a pension is promised for as long as needed, to give it is of little use, one of its chief values being that it relieves the mind of the recipient from worry, as well as his body from hunger. Dream and uncertainty of the future cause the greatest suffering to the homeless aged. But no one who has not personally tried to secure the contributions necessary to pension an old man can realize how hard is the task. The fact that an amount must be paid regularly and for a period of time which cannot possibly be foretold, usually makes even near relatives of old men hesitate to pledge themselves, and persons upon whom they have no claim will not usually subscribe to such funds at all. Even 50 cents or one dollar a month, when it must be pledged for an indefinite length of time, seems to most persons too much of an obligation to assume, but there must be at least 16 one-dollar-a-month pledges before even a small pension can be guaranteed.

We found, too, that it was much more difficult to persuade persons to be financially responsible for the care of the old—particularly old men—than it was of the young. . . . This difference is, of course, to be expected, since work for the young has elements of hope and interest which must always be lacking in work for the old. Perhaps this is also the reason why homes and institutions for children are numerous in all parts of the country and are sometimes in excess of existing needs, while those for old people are so comparatively few that actual suffering results.

• • •

When in trying to secure adequate aid for self-respecting old men we found that there were neither relatives nor friends who could be interested in their behalf, and when because of breaking health the men were no longer able to work, we invariably were confronted with a problem which in most cases we were unable to solve because the lack of institutions made it impossible for us to offer the men the sort of care they should have had. As before stated, there were a few men whom we did not hesitate to send out to Dunning and who were quite willing to go there.

New York: Survey Associates, pp. 13–50.

LOSERS OF THE AMERICAN DREAM: NELS ANDERSON'S *THE HOBO*

Nels Anderson's 1923 book on the transient is the first important study of a group of people who by the 1930s would quadruple in number. The following excerpts focus on aged transients and those with mental and physical handicaps and illnesses. Anderson presents a case study of an elderly man much like the old paisano in *The Red Pony* who resists being taken care of in an almshouse and is unable to subsist on his own. From his writing it is clear that there were many men like Lennie among the homeless drifters he observed.

FROM NELS ANDERSON, *THE HOBO* (1923)

[Old Men:]

Many old men in the tramp class are not able to work and are too independent to go to the almshouse. Some of them have spent their lives on the road. These old, homeless men usually find their way to the larger cities. Unlike the younger men they have no dreams and no longer burn with the desire to travel. Many have been self-supporting until they were overtaken by senility. It is pitiable to see an old man tottering along the streets living a hand-to-mouth existence.

18. J. is an old man who lives in a cheap hotel on South Desplains Street, where a few cents a day will house him. He is seventy-two, very bent and gray. Once he was picked up on the street in winter and sent to the hospital where he remained a day or two and was transferred to the poor house at Oak Forest. He ran away from the poor house two years ago and has managed to live. He seldom gets more than a block or two from his lodging. Even today (1923) he may be seen on a cold day shivering without an overcoat on Madison Street. He is a good beggar and manages to get from fifty cents to a dollar a day from the "boys" on the "stem." Sometimes during the warm weather he makes excursions of three to five blocks away on begging tours. He is exceedingly feeble and walking that distance is hard work for him. Work is out of the question. There are very few jobs that he could manage.

This case is typical. During the summer time, when it is possible to sit outdoors in comfort, numbers of old men may be found in groups on the pavements or in the parks. In winter they are too much occupied seeking food and shelter.

[Handicapped:]
   The physically handicapped and industrially inefficient individuals are numerous among the homeless men. The handicap is, in part at least, the reason of their presence in that class. Competition with able-bodied workers forces them into the scrap heap. (69–70)

• • •

The proportion of feebleminded is popularly supposed to be higher among the migratory and casual laborer than in the general population. In the earlier studies, only the most obvious cases of mental defect were noted. Mrs. Solenberger by common-sense observation or medical examinations found only eighty-nine of the one thousand she examined to be feeble-minded, epileptic, or insane.[1]

• • •

The defects in personality commonly found in the cases of homeless men studied in Chicago are those noted by the students of vagabondage and unemployment, namely, feeblemindedness, constitutional inferiority, emotional instability, and egocentricity. In a survey of 100 cases of unemployment which had been received as patients in the Boston Psychopathic Hospital, Dr. Herman M. Adler found that 43 fell into the class of *paranoid personality* (egocentricity). The next largest group of 35 cases was assigned to the class of *inadequate personality* (mentally defective or feeble-minded). The remaining cases, 22 in number, were diagnosed as *emotionally unstable personality*. An analysis of the months employed per case showed that the emotionally unstable group averages 50 months to each job; and the paranoid group 10.6 months to each job.[2]
   Many individuals not feeble-minded find their way into the group of casual and migratory workers by reason of other defects of personality, for example, emotional instability and egocentricity. Among transient laborers the very great turnover cannot be entirely accounted for by industrial conditions. Much of their shifting from scene to scene is indicative of their emotional instability and restlessness.

• • •

[Physically Defective:]
   Mrs. Alice W. Solenberger found that two-thirds of her 1,000 cases were

either physically or mentally defective. Of these, 627 men and boys were suffering from a total of 722 physical and mental deficiencies.[3]

Condition	Instances
Insanity	52
Feeblemindedness	19
Epilepsy	18
Paralysis	40
Other nervous disorders	21
Tuberculosis	93
Rheumatism	37
Venereal diseases	21
Other infectious diseases	15
Heart disease	14
Disorders of organs other than heart	19
Crippled, maimed, or deformed; from birth or accident	168
Rupture	11
Cancer	6
Blind, including partly blind	43
Deaf, including partly deaf	14
Defective health through use of drugs and drink	16
Defective health from lack of nourishment and other causes	24
Convalescent	33
Aged	35
All other diseases and defects	7
Doubtful	16
Total instances	722
Total number of different men in defective health or condition	627

She tells us that of the 22 more or less permanently handicapped, 106 men had been entirely self-supporting before their injuries while 127 were entirely dependent after injury.

A careful study of 100 homeless men made in the Municipal Lodging House of New York City by F. C. Lauback showed the following defects.

Tuberculosis	7
Venereal	26
Bronchial	4
Feeble	14
Senile	16
Deformed	4
Maimed	14
Malnutrition	13
Poor sight	9
Poor hearing	1
Impediment of speech	2
Physically sound	28

Laubach's 100 cases were selected from more than 400 men. They represented the 100 who remained longest to be examined (perhaps the 100 the least able to get away). He found 28 per cent able-bodied while Mrs. Solenberger reported 37.3 per cent without observable defects. That this per cent of defectives is high for more unselected groups will be shown by the following extract from the report of the Municipal Lodging House of New York City for 1915.

> . . . Fifteen hundred men were studied by a staff of fifteen investigators. At the same time a medical examination of two thousand men was conducted by fifteen medical examiners. This investigation represented the first large attempt in America to find out about the men who take refuge in a municipal lodging house. . . .
>
> Of the 2,000 men who were given a medical examination, 1,774, or approximately 9 out of every 10, were, according to the adjudgments of the examining physicians, physically able to work. Twelve hundred and forty-seven, or 62 per cent of the total, were considered physically able to do regular hard manual labor; 254, or 18 per cent, to do medium hard work; and 173, or 9 per cent, to do light work only. Two hundred and twenty-six, 1 out of every 10, were adjudged physically unable to work.[4]

This investigation showed that in a lean year, when many men were out of work, a large proportion of the lodging-house population is composed of handicapped men. The physical condition of 400 tramps interviewed by the writer is not so much in contradiction as in supplement to the foregoing studies.[5] Only men in transit were tabulated. Nearly all of them were the typical migratory workers or hobos. Observation was limited to apparent defects that would hinder in a noticeable manner the working capacity of the men.

Senile	6
Maimed	8
Eye lost or partly blind	5
Eye trouble	5
Venereal disease	1
Partly paralyzed	2
Tuberculosis	2
Feeble-minded	7
Chronic poor health	4
Impediment of speech	2
Temporarily injured	4
Oversized or undersized	4

These 50 defects were distributed among 48 persons.

Subtracting those who could be classed mentally defective, we have but forty-one persons who were apparently physically handicapped. It will be noted that the percentage of the aged is considerably lower than the previous tables show. The same is true of the maimed and injured. They were all men who were able to "get over the road." One of the maimed men had lost an arm while the two others had each lost a foot.

Eye trouble was listed separately because these were ailments that were passing. Three of the men had weak eyes and this condition had been aggravated by train riding and loss of sleep. One man had been gassed in the army and his eyes suffered from the wind and bright light. Only one man admitted that he was suffering from a venereal disease.

Both men suffering from tuberculosis were miners. Both had been in hospitals for treatment. One of them was in a precarious condition. The men listed as oversized and undersized might be properly considered handicapped. Two of them were uncomfortably fat while the other two were conspicuously under weight and height.

The Hobo's Health on the Job

Often the seasonal work sought by the migratory worker is located in out-of-the-way places or with little or no medical or sanitary supervision. Sometimes there are not even tents for the men to sleep in. Life and work in the open, so conducive to health on bright, warm days, involves exposure in cold and stormy weather. In the northwest, where rain is so abundant that workers suffer considerably from exposure, strikes have even been called to enforce demands for warm, dry bunkhouses.

In addition to the exposure to the elements there are other hazards the migratory and casual workers run. On most of his jobs, whether in the woods, the swamps, in the sawmills, or the mines and quarries, in the harvest, on bridges or on the highways, the hobo faces danger. Since he is in the habit of working only a few days at a time, a well-paying, hazardous job appeals to him. The not infrequent accidents are serious since few of these foot-loose men carry insurance.

Seasonal labor generally consists of hard work like shoveling or lifting and carrying heavy loads. Only men who can do hard work are wanted. Not much so-called "light work" aside from a few jobs in kitchens, in stables, or about camps is open to the transient. Many homeless men are not physically able to do eight or ten hours' hard labor without suffering. They are often weak from eating poor food or from dissipation. Even if they go on a job with their minds made up to remain one or two months they are often obliged to leave after a few days. Often the hobo works on jobs where there is no medical attention. Sometimes, where the job includes large numbers of men, a physician is hired to go from camp to camp. He is usually known as a "pill peddler" and all he pretends to do is give first aid to the injured and treat passing ailments. Serious cases he sends to the hospital.

Big industrial organizations usually carry some sort of medical insurance and in some cases accident insurance. This system of workingmen's compensation for industrial accidents is maintained sometimes by fees taken from the pay of the men, sometimes entirely by the employer. The accident compensation, the hospital, and medical privileges apply only to ailments and injuries caused by his work.

The food the hobo receives on the job is not always palatable, nor does it always come up to the requirements of a balanced diet or the caloric needs of a workingman. In the business of feeding the men, considerable exploitation enters which the men are powerless to prevent. The boarding contracts are often let to boarding companies that agree to feed the men and furnish bunks for prices ranging (since the war) from five to eight dollars a week. For the privilege of boarding the workers, they agree to keep the gangs filled. Often in the West the men furnish their own beds, but private "bundle beds" are passing. Some companies furnish good beds, but the general rule is to supply a tick that may be filled with straw and a couple of quilts which are charged to the worker until he returns them. These quilts and blankets are often used again and again by different men without being cleaned during a whole season.

Several boarding companies maintain free employment agencies in Chicago, well known to the hobo and generally disliked. The chief complaint against them is that in hard times, when men are plentiful, there is a tendency to drop on the quality and the quantity of the food. In such an event the monotony of the menu and the unsavory manner in which food is prepared is a scandal in Hoboland. However, all complaints against boarding companies are not due to bad food. Poor cooking is another ground for much dissatisfaction. Efficient camp cooks are rare and too high priced for the average boarding company.

• • •

[Handicapped:]

The Problem of Health

Disease, physical disability, and insanitary living conditions seem to be, as things are, the natural and inevitable consequences of the migratory risk-taking and irregular life of the homeless man. These effects of his work and life upon his physical constitution will be considered by the most appalling of all the problems affecting the hobo and the tramp. Municipal provisions and philanthropic effort have been and will continue to be directed to the treatment of his diseases and defects and to the improvement of his living conditions. The efficiency of the homeless man as a worker and his chance of regaining his lost economic and social status depend upon his physical rehabilitation. A clearing house for the homeless man when established should, therefore, include as one of its activities facilities for diagnosis of the needs, medical, vocational, social, of each individual.

The living conditions of the homeless man, although revolting to the public, are intolerable to him, chiefly as a symbol of his degradation. Lodging-house sanitation and personal hygiene are of minor import, in his thinking, as compared with working conditions, or, for that matter, with the problems of his social and political status.

1. *One Thousand Homeless Men*, pp. 88–89.
2. Herman M. Adler, "Unemployment and Personality—A Study of Psychopathic Cases," *Mental Hygiene*, I (January 1917), 16–17.
3. Alice W. Solenberger, *One Thousand Homeless Men*, p. 36.

4. *Report of the Advisory Social Service Committee of the Municipal Lodging House*, pp. 9–11. New York City: September, 1915.

5. This unpublished study of 400 tramps was made while riding freight trains from Salt Lake City, Utah, to Chicago in the summer of 1921. All the cases tabulated were cases in transit. A large part of them were men who regularly beat their way about the country. Document 115.

Chicago: University of Chicago Press, pp. 69–136.

LOSERS IN PARADISE: CAREY MCWILLIAMS'
ILL FARES THE LAND

Carey McWilliams, who was often named along with John Steinbeck as a man dangerous to California agriculture because of his courageous writings in support of poor farm workers, first caught the attention of the country with *Factories in the Field* (1939), an exposé of the living and working conditions of those by whose labor Americans were fed. In the following excerpt he outlines the inadequate labor standards in United States agriculture. Of special pertinence to Steinbeck is McWilliams' observation of the extent to which farm workers are excluded from workers' compensation as well as the reasons for their exclusion. Also note the dangers involved in farm labor to which men like Candy are exposed.

FROM CAREY MCWILLIAMS, *ILL FARES THE LAND* (1942)

The cotton-picking army is thoroughly mechanized; it is an army on wheels. The typical unit of transportation is the open, or stake, truck. Wherever the contractor system prevails, trucks are the principal means of transportation. In the truck will usually be loaded a crew of from fifty to sixty pickers together with a large amount of miscellaneous equipment. In an accident at McAllen, Texas, in 1940, 44 Mexicans riding in a truck were injured; 29 were killed and, of these, 11 were children under the age of sixteen. The truck itself had a cab on the front and a body behind. There were solid sides on the body and the end-gates were closed. Across the top of the body a tarpaulin had been placed, so that the 44 workers in the back of the truck could not see out. Accidents of this type are, of course, quite common; they occur every season, and the contractors seldom, if ever, carry insurance.

. . .

The best characterization of farm laborers, as a class, that I have ever read is that by Mr. N. C. Durham. He refers to them as "economic half-castes"—cut off from the possibility of farm ownership and denied the meager protection given almost every worker in industry. Not only are farm workers "economic half-castes" but they are "second-class citizens," for they are denied many of the rights and privileges of American citizenship.

The first thing to do, therefore, to aid this group is to remove the disabilities under which they now suffer. While some qualifications might be noted for absolute accuracy, nevertheless it can be said generally that agricultural labor has no legislative protection at present in this country. Farm workers are "exempt" from our entire scheme of social legislation, state and federal. Historically several reasons were urged to establish the precedent for exempting agriculture from social legislation. It was said that agricultural labor did not need this protection; that the industrial revolution had not arrived in agriculture; that farmers were subject to special hazards, such as weather conditions, which made them a legitimate object of legislative favoritism. But the "real reasons for the exemption of farm laborers," as Professor Willard C. Fisher pointed out in 1917, "are political, nothing else. Farm laborers are not organized into unions, nor have they other means of bringing their wishes to the attention of legislators." Most of our social legislation, in fact, has been enacted as the result of a political "deal" between organized labor and the farm groups. The basis of this deal has always been: we, the farm representatives, will not object to this legislation, if you, the representatives of organized labor, will agree to exempt agricultural employees.

Today it has become imperative for us to establish some fair labor standards in agricultural employment. Consider, for example, the matter of workmen's compensation insurance. Only four states treat agricultural employment the same as nonagricultural employment so far as compensation for industrial injuries is concerned. Yet what are the industrial facts? As early as 1911 Mr. Don Lescohier pointed out that the substitution of power machinery for hand labor had made agriculture a hazardous industry. "Much of the machinery used," he wrote, "is far more dangerous than that used in most factories, for sufficient attention has not been paid to guarding it." Not a single state has issued a code of safety regulations especially designed to apply to farm machinery. More people are killed today in the course of farm work than in any other one industry. Occupational deaths in agriculture were estimated at 4300 in 1939—over one fourth of the total fatalities for all industries. In 1936, 6100 agricultural workers received permanent disabilities and 253,000 were temporarily disabled. These figures, in my opinion, are ultraconservative. They do not include fatalities on the road and hundreds of workers are constantly receiving injuries while moving from one area to another. A great many occupational injuries are never reported in agricultural employment. Also, occupational diseases are quite common in agriculture. Today there is no reason for the exclusion of agricultural workers from the protection of workmen's compensation laws. "A leg injury," it has been said, "from a cutting tool used in harvesting is just as disabling as one sustained in a factory."

Boston: Little, Brown, pp. 330–390.

HOPE IN NEW FAMILIES: WILLIAM T. AND DOROTHY E. CROSS' *NEWCOMERS AND NOMADS IN CALIFORNIA*

In 1937 the whole world knew of the plight of the aged, the handicapped, and the injured farm workers of the Depression. In their study of the action being taken at the state and federal level, the Crosses point out one way in which elderly and handicapped workers were dealing with their situation of hopelessness: some were forming cooperatives or small units in which they could live together and assist each other—exactly as George, Lennie, Candy, and, for a brief moment, Crooks think of doing.

FROM WILLIAM T. CROSS AND DOROTHY E. CROSS, *NEWCOMERS AND NOMADS IN CALIFORNIA* (1937)

Agricultural and industrial colonies, it may be recalled, have sprung up in earlier periods of American history. They have been known generally for their peculiarities as cults. Many, if not most, of these groups have represented co-operative enterprises on the part of a number of middle-aged persons who were discouraged with the prevailing ways of gaining a livelihood and who, having little or no savings, feared to face old age alone. Most of the men over forty-five years of age met by the field investigators on the road, in California, particularly the skilled craftsmen, had about given up hope of finding work.

Men of this sort, in the earlier co-operative experiments, appear to have discovered advantages in joining hands. The tenets they adopted gave motivation to individual lives and increased the coherence of the group. The simpler standards of the new life were a welcome and an economical substitute for the ways of the outside world. There was greater stability and security under the common roof. It may be in the public interest, during the "long pull" out of the recent depression, to encourage people of the type that comes to shelters to form co-operative agricultural colonies.

Stanford: Stanford University Press, pp. 88–89.

HOMELESS IN PARADISE: AN INTERVIEW WITH SALVATION ARMY BRIGADIER LUTHER SMITH

Luther Smith joined the Salvation Army in 1935 and was commissioned and ordained as a lieutenant in 1936. He has had extensive experience working with the elderly and handicapped poor in many parts of North and South America: Georgia, North and South Carolina, Tennessee, Oklahoma, Florida, Louisiana, Honduras, Guatemala, Costa Rica, the Dominican Republic, and Mexico. The following excerpts, taken from an interview with him on his home base in Birmingham, Alabama, include his memories of working with the homeless during his sixty-year career.

FROM AN INTERVIEW WITH BRIGADIER LUTHER SMITH OF
BIRMINGHAM, ALABAMA (1996)

Interviewer (hereafter identified as CJ): I am particularly interested in your experience with homeless elderly and retarded men. Let me ask you to please identify yourself for me.

Smith: I'm Brigadier Luther Smith of the Salvation Army. I became an officer in 1936 so this is my sixtieth year.

CJ: Where did you get started?

Smith: In Anniston. I was a member of Parker Memorial Church. I was going with a good looking redheaded girl. One Sunday morning in church she asked me, "Would you like to go to a Salvation Army meeting?" Well wherever she was interested in going, that's where my interests lay. So we went. It was in the Rex Theatre. The Army would often rent places like that for open meetings. And these were cadets. There were seven of them from our school for officers' training in Atlanta where our seminary would be. Within thirty minutes, before any preaching, I said, "Gosh, that's what I want to do." These men had a sense of direction, a sense of joy, a sense of feeling that what they were doing was important. And I said that's what I want to do. I could have stayed in the Baptist Church; I could have gone in my father's business, but I think—what in time would have happened if I hadn't gone to that meeting. By the way, *she* married an undertaker. So that's another story. So that's the way I got in the army.

CJ: And you spent most of your life in this area?

Smith: In the fifteen Southern states. In Georgia, Tennessee, Washington, D.C., Texas, Mexico, and back to Oklahoma.

CJ: So you've had a full range of experience?

Smith: I've spent a lot of time in Central and South America.

CJ: I'm interested in the men you saw in the thirties and forties—whether or not they had some sense of the American Dream, of comfort— even plenty—some hope that they could achieve that dream.

Smith: Well, you see most of them had problems with substance abuse.

CJ: Even back in those days?

Smith: Yes.

CJ: Primarily alcohol abuse?

Smith: Yes, alcohol in those days. And of course what they were trying to do was to get a roof over their head that night. For instance, I know, all things being equal, where I am going to spend the night. I've got a wife; I've got a house; I've got a shower; I've got a refrigerator. I can call Sears to come out and fix a broken appliance. You know what I mean. *These* people—a transient was a man on his way from Atlanta to New Orleans to get a job. And all he needed was over-night care, food and so on, and next day he was on his way to get a job. Now we have always had three or four hundred homeless men who have been alcoholics primarily. Now about forty percent of them are having trouble with drugs. So there is a lot of that.

CJ: Did they seem to be—and again I'm speaking of the thirties and for-ties—did these homeless men have a sense that there was no way out?

Smith: Yes.

CJ: Did any of them have the notion that at sometime they—

Smith: I think they felt that they were completely imprisoned by their addiction. I don't think they did much good thinking. Such a man ordinarily has a short fuse. He's a fragile person. For instance, you take—you have some relationship to an employee. And you say to him, "Joe, you know, we really need to get this done," or "I've got a light up here that really needs fixing." And he says to me, "I can't do *everything*!" And you know that within a week he's going to be gone. Because, you know, he's getting on edge. So, to get back, you were asking if these men had a dream. But their dream was so beclouded with alcohol that you couldn't really figure them. Now, back in those days, we had a home for transients, for homeless men, and so forth up the street. And at that time we had a wood yard out in the back. And a man that would come for over night care, or for groceries or whatever, we would say, "Now there's a wood pile; you need to work a couple of hours," or something like that. You see, that's not being mean. That's really being helpful. The problem is we don't have enough work for people to do. Now there are some people who are low-down and lazy, but many of them are hard-working, nice people to work with, but they just have the sword of Damocles hanging over their head and they have a real problem.

CJ: So they're just living from day to day? They're not thinking: "One day I'll get out of this. I'll have a house of my own."

Smith: Right. There's a program here that provides health care for the homeless. And they have a vehicle that goes around. And they did a study. I think that 27% of the homeless have mental or psychological problems. There are people who have psychological problems and they just cannot work in any structured situation. And then you have the drug abuse problems. We had a man for years who lived under a bridge here. So the Salvation Army had a disaster van that would go to places—for instance grates where men were sleeping over the grates to keep warm. And we would carry food to them and so forth. We were coming to the end of that program and somebody said to him, "Lloyd, you know, really, you ought to go up to the Army and maybe something can be worked out for you." So he decided he would. So he came. And now he is a member of the Salvation Army, wears a uniform, and is a representative of the army. We recently had a meeting with about a thousand people who were given statistics about the work of the Army, and Lloyd got up and said, "You have heard the statistics; I am one of those statistics." And then he told his story. And let me tell you that made the difference. Here is a man who has been completely dependent and now he's independent. He has a little truck that he drives. He has a little apartment that he lives in. And his life has just changed completely. And you see, when I began, the transient was the single man. Now the transient may be a man, his wife and two children who are sleeping in a car.

CJ: When did that happen?

Smith: Well, the homelessness is a—when a family gets in trouble, they often have a brother or a sister or a mother or a father they can go to live with for a short period of time while they get on their feet. Some of them have not been able to get on their feet that quickly.

Another thing when you have a house full and your cousin moves in, it gets a little cozy. It is difficult. Now, we have transitional housing. We have twelve units. We used to say to the man, "You go down this way to a men's unit," and we sent the wife and children to a women's unit. But now we think that a family in trouble needs to be together. We say to them, "Now if you're interested in taking charge of your life"—we say to them "We will furnish you roof, clothes, food—not for three days—we will provide this for several months, if necessary," while they get job training or a GED or that type of thing. Maybe it's literacy training. And we help them to get a job. And the money they make is *their* money. So the idea is for them to save their money and get an apartment and pay the deposits and all this kind of thing. So we are trying to get them into a situation where they are in charge of their own life.

CJ: In your experience—and you've mentioned the substance abuse— but aside from that, why did most men—single men end up homeless?

Smith: Well, in the thirties and forties—the government paid the Salvation Army—I believe it was fifty cents a day to house these men. Because you see we had *thousands* of people who were out of a job.

CJ: In the thirties?

Smith: There weren't any jobs. So they hoboed back and forth on a train. And if a man lost his job here—and there wasn't any job, especially in rural areas. Farmers—when you worked on a farm—the farmer didn't have any money to pay you. So a lot of the people, black and white, went north where there was the industrial area where they could get jobs. But there were very few opportunities to get a job. And when a man could get a job, he'd get it and he'd basically hold onto it. And send for his family. See these—this thing, when I am willing to work and I can't get a job, man, I say, the system has failed me. This is not right. And so there were few jobs. We are seeing something of the same thing now with all the downsizing of companies. A man may have worked for a company for thirty years and someone has bought the company and they are downsizing, and you have done everything you can do and you've been a good employee but the job isn't there. And that takes it out of you. That's tough. But the modern situation with homelessness is a lot of that, but homelessness is again—when you take a homeless person with psychological or mental problems and add to that the substance abuser, you've got 75 to 85% of your people.

CJ: Did you have in the thirties transient workers coming through—workers that followed the fields?

Smith: Oh, oh yeah. Now that's been a great program. Now you've had some people in this country taking advantage of them, putting them in shacks and just terrible, terrible, terrible. But most of them are so anxious to work. See, we have jobs today that the average person just would not do. And you have migratory workers. In the old days, it was cotton picking, and now we have fruit and vegetables all up and down the coast. And we have wheat—people following that. And it's tough. But now we do have much better conditions. Because we have the health department monitoring the situation. But we have always had migratory workers. Let me tell you a quick story. I was stationed in Mexico City. And one of our friends called us and told us that he had just discovered a new mother with twins living in a cave. I went down and found it and talked to the father. He was a poor, poor man and had this wife who had twins. And I asked him what could you do if you had the money to set you up, and he said he would be able to sell kerosene—oil. There's a bunch of people living in caves and living in shanty towns around the area so I thought: that looks like that's do-able. So we got an oil company to cooperate. But when I checked back in about two weeks, his wife said he was gone. I was absolutely furious. He messed up. He was gone about two months. And one day he walked in the office. What he had done—he said, "I could get the oil up there but the people couldn't provide me with oil when I needed it so the idea of the oil just didn't work." So he had gone to the States and do you know during that time, he had sent every cent—because you know migratory workers—they fed them and housed them so he didn't have any expenses so he sent his money back to his wife. So he went up there and worked for a few months and he got enough money to provide for his family for the year. People do what they have to do. His intentions were good and he was a willing worker. Migratory workers are willing to work and will work long long hours.

CJ: In the thirties, as you say, many of these were single men, men travelling alone.

Smith: Oh, yes. Most of them were. There were some travelling with families. Sometimes the wife works, sometimes the children go to the fields with them. Out in California and in Texas they have some real problems because of large numbers, but some of them are hard working people, some of them are good people, the salt of the earth. The migratory worker was part of the system.

CJ: In your experience, were there any, or significant numbers of mentally retarded men among the homeless?

Smith: It's hard to tell. You take Lennie in *Of Mice and Men*—he was surely typical. In any situation where you have large numbers of men, you're bound to have those that are just not normal. And there would be in any situation like that—we had in those days what we do not have now—the extended family. So that, say, the grand-mother would take care of the children or the retarded child.

CJ: Back then in the thirties, if they had no family to care for them, what were their options?

Smith: They had very few options, but I think we had a society that was a caring society. They had hearts. And I think they always had people who would care for them though it was extremely difficult. I have known of situations like that and if they do not have anyone—for instance, there was what were called poor farms and people would go to the poor farms, but they were under-funded and there were not enough of them. Now, of course, we have social security, and social security supplement so now most people have a little money. Here in Birmingham, we had a program where institutions would take the social security money of people like Lennie and then look after them. And it was a good, good program.

CJ: Often I have read that caring for the mentally retarded man was so difficult, because they would not stay in these houses.

Smith: That's right. Many of the people—I remember interviewing a woman under the bridges here and asking her if she would not come up here to get shelter and food, but she wasn't interested. If you urged, she would come with you but she would not stay. She had mental problems. And you have other people who are living a life-style like that and they are not interested in a structured environ-ment. You will be interested in knowing that 200 people will sleep under a Salvation Army roof tonight.

CJ: Let's focus for a minute on elderly men—homeless elderly men before social security.

Smith: There were those people—there was an elderly man who was not related to anyone—he would go from place to place and he wouldn't make any serious contribution in this farm setting. He could talk to you in a normal way. But he really didn't have it. He would never stay at any place for any period of time. He could kind of sense when he was wearing out his welcome. And he and others like him were at the mercy of these basically kind-hearted farm people who had no real obligation to them. But such elderly men were really in a bind.

You see they had no family themselves and no one had any obligation to them. And so sometimes it was extremely difficult for them.

CJ: Were there many elderly workers left unprotected by any social programs?

Smith: Yes, there was no social program that I know of except in industrial areas there were places where they could go and stay. But the elderly man has no contribution to make and he's at the sufferance of others. And there were so few systems that could accommodate anyone like that. And I would say that a person that was elderly or handicapped, they were in real, real trouble. It's so tragic. You take a person that's willing to work—we used to say to a person, son if you get a job and you work forty hours a week, you can provide for your family. But now, you see a man working at entry level wage now—if you're working at McDonald's or working at Wal-Mart, you know they won't let you work the full forty hours. So now if a man and his wife work they can kind of get by.

CJ: What was the daily life like of the homeless elderly man in the thirties?

Smith: He was interested in getting someplace to lay his head at night. You see, he wasn't thinking about the long range—what are my goals? His goal was to find a place to stay tonight. And his goal was to get food. And it meant going from trash can to trash can. It meant staying at the Salvation Army for one night, going to the mission for one night, going to an aunt's house for one night. Doing anything he could. Cause he had no long range goals. Everything was very short range. I mean how am I going to survive the night.

CJ: What kind of circumstance would leave an old man homeless?

Smith: What you basically have is someone with very limited skills. They may have been raised on a farm. Might be good behind a plow, but when he gets to Birmingham, there are not many jobs to plow. And he would get a job as a janitor, if he could, or an elevator operator. And you take for instance both white and black. I remember back in the old days, a black man had to be a teacher or a preacher or an elevator operator. White people had many more options but there were not many more jobs. And that, take for instance, I was stationed out in Oklahoma and those people went to California. People from around here went to Detroit because they could get those jobs up there and some could make it up there and some couldn't.

CJ: In the thirties and forties, for elderly people who were homeless and alone, was communal living ever an answer?

Smith: I don't think so. Communal living came into vogue in the sixties where they had these communes. But these people—you take the hobo—and the hobo jungle beside the railroad and they'd get some cans and they'd go up and down the street and they had a way of marking a fence post to let others know, this lady will give you something to eat, or will give you work, and cut grass or something. And there's nothing wrong in that. If you came to me and I said my lawn needed cutting. Well that's a fair exchange for food.

CJ: And they never tended to form groups that would help each other out?

Smith: No. But yet there again, in the hobo jungle, they would sometimes go together to make a meal. They'd get a bottle and share that. And wake up the next morning with a big head and without shoes, even without clothes. Because there were predators that would do that to other people.

CJ: And I suppose especially the very old people?

Smith: Absolutely, they were the victims. Defenseless. Just like in a prison system. You've got those that are in charge and those that are not in charge. It was an awful, awful thing.

CJ: Were blacks and whites just as segregated in that kind of transient situation as they were, say, in southern society as a whole?

Smith: Yes, and yet in our society we are much more inclusive than we were back then. But in those days, you still had the segregation. The white man would sit over there and the black man over here, but they might give him some of the food. And in fact, he may have brought something to put in the soup. But there was still segregation, because everyone was looking for someone to look down on and the poor black man was somebody that everybody could thank god they were not like that.

CJ: Do you recall there being any particular lines of work that would leave an elderly man destitute?

Smith: Well the unions were a serious factor in protecting workers.

CJ: The unions beginning to be a serious factor when? in the fifties or in the thirties?

Smith: In the thirties and forties you had the organization, but they came into their strength in the fifties. They were very strong.

CJ: Farm workers weren't particularly represented though, were they?

Smith: No not at all, not at all. Now you have Chavez out in California, but I know in this part of the country, farm workers were not represented at all.

CJ: Related to the instability of the life?

Smith: Oh, yes. And with a farmer, he can do everything that a farmer can do, the farm can still be wiped out. Farm work ceased to be viable and these workers began to migrate to the cities. Individual small farms were less common.

CJ: In the thirties and forties, were there significant numbers of people who were out of work because of illnesses and injuries?

Smith: There were some, but I think by and large, you know we didn't have an OSHA [Occupational Safety and Health Administration] in those days. And much of the work was very dangerous. Companies had a moral obligation, but they did not have a legal obligation to injured workers. And you know there are some people—for example, in the textile mills, a person could get injured very easily and sometimes the mills would take care of these people unofficially and there were sometimes those extended families to take care of them.

CJ: I wanted to ask you one other thing about the elderly destitute—the poor. What sorts of work were found for them to do?

Smith: Well, very little. Sometimes you even found men acting as baby-sitters. You know grandad type persons and he may not even be related to the family he worked for. But you see, the elderly, both male and female, wanted to do something and they would see something that needed to be done and they would just do it. It was a make-do situation. If I came to your house and was living in your house, I wanted to help. In the old days, an elderly man may carry the water to field workers. That was a valid job. It might be a sixty-year-old man and there weren't many over sixty because people didn't live as long in those days.

CJ: I suppose you would say that the biggest change in the lives of the elderly poor came with social security.

Smith: Oh, absolutely.

CJ: How might you compare the life of someone living before social security with someone living afterward?

Smith: Well they had no rights, no call on anyone. You're talking about a poor person among poor people. So many of them were hurting badly. Some people will tell you that social security is the ruin of the nation. Let me tell you if you don't have any money coming in, you go with your hat in your hand anywhere you go. I can't think of anything worse than that. Now a person gets social security. There are boarding houses which provide food and shelter and medical care for that social security check. This is where people live together. And that's not a bad arrangement. If I only had my social security, and I needed basic essentials, while there is a certain amount of exploitation, more than likely it is the best thing you can think of for that man or woman.

CJ: So the whole scope of the Salvation Army has expanded tremendously since the thirties when you got involved.

Smith: Oh, yes. It used to be just a transient bureau. I have seen rules elsewhere that specified that help would be provided for one night in thirty days and no more. But what can happen in one night? You need more time. All that is is a night. But we can help people get on their feet in what we call a pay dorm. For seven dollars a night, a person can stay here and have an address and food and shelter and use of a telephone, the idea being that a person can get a job and save money to eventually get an apartment and become independent. Many people work out well on that system.

NOTES

1. A. F. Tredgold, *Mental Deficiency* (New York: William Wood and Co., 1922), p. 201.

2. *Mental Retardation: Past and Present* (Washington, D.C.: President's Committee on Retardation, January 1977), p. 21.

TOPICS FOR WRITTEN OR ORAL EXPLORATION

1. The grandfather in *The Red Pony* contended that he hated the Pacific Ocean because it ended the frontier. Discuss the question of what frontiers are left to satisfy an active person's dream of adventure. Are some physical and some intellectual?

2. Write an essay on the shape of the American Dream in your own family, starting with one of your grandparents, then your parents, then you. What changes have occurred over the generations?

3. Interview someone over seventy-five years old. Ask them about their view of adventure when they were young. How important was adventure to them? Did they pursue a dream of adventure? If so, what was it and how did it shape their life?

4. How does the generation gap (as between the grandfather and his son-in-law) appear now in the 1990s?

5. Discuss why the very young often seem to relate more positively to the elderly than the generation between them.

6. Write a personal essay about your own relationship with an older person when you were about Jody's age.

7. Discuss in an essay or in class the following: Does Candy have any real choice about allowing his dog to be shot? Is there anything he could have or should have done?

8. What, if anything, does Curley's wife have in common with Lennie, Candy, and Crooks?

9. Write a research paper on the present recommended treatment of the mentally handicapped in our own society.

10. As a research project, try to determine which elderly men or women "fall through the cracks" in terms of social security benefits.

11. Invite a panel of experts who deal with the elderly poor, including one elderly person him- or herself, to address the class and answer carefully prepared questions. Consider not only the problems of health and survival, but the burden of public attitudes and psychological difficulties.

SUGGESTIONS FOR FURTHER READING

Allen, Frederick Lewis. *The Big Change: America Transforms Itself, 1900–1950.* New York: Harper and Brothers, 1952.

Axinn, June, and Herman Levin. *Social Welfare: A History of the American Response to Need.* New York: Longman, 1982.

Brown, J. Douglas. *An American Philosophy of Social Security: Evaluation and Issues*. Princeton: Princeton University Press, 1972.

Croly, Herbert. *The Promise of American Life*. New York: Macmillan, 1912.

Epstein, Abraham. *Facing Old Age*. New York: Alfred A. Knopf, 1922.

Garraty, John A. *The Great Depression*. New York: Anchor Books, 1987.

Katz, Michael B. *In the Shadow of the Poorhouse*. New York: Basic Books, 1986.

Knepper, Max. "Scrambled Eggs in California." *Current History* 51 (October 1939): 58–60.

Scheerenberger, R. C. *A History of Mental Retardation*. Baltimore: Brookes, 1983.

Smith, J. David. *Minds Made Feeble*. Rockville, Md.: Aspen Systems Corp., 1985.

Young, Donald Ramsey. *American Minority Peoples: A Study in Racial and Cultural Conflicts in the United States*. New York: Harper Brothers, 1932.

6

The American Dream in a Mexican Setting

Although *The Pearl* is frequently read primarily as a legend, the political nature of the story is apparent in several ways: in the contrasts between rich and poor; the issue of race and caste; the role of the clerical, professional, and business classes in suppressing the poor; and the impossibility of the poor ever realizing a dream of a better life.

Steinbeck's story opens with the marked contrasts between the lives of the poor and the very rich. Kino and Juana live with their child, Coyotito, in a brush house with a dirt floor, where a single room serves as the couple's bedroom, the nursery, and the kitchen. They cook in an open pit in the same room where the whole family sleeps. Every morning of their lives their breakfast consists of corncakes, sauce, and pulque, which in its usual state was a cheap alcoholic drink. This Kino drinks several times a day.

Contrasted to the brush house, which the wind can blow through, and the simple (one might even say inadequate) fare they eat are the residence and food of the wealthy. The rich people in town live not in brush houses, but in houses of stone and plaster. The doctor's house is enclosed by a wall and has a gate with an iron door knocker, while Kino's wall is made of brush and his floor is a dirt one crawling with ants. The doctor's white wall encloses exotic plants and a fountain. His bedchamber has a high bed and other heavy furniture.

While Kino eats with his fingers, the doctor's food is served on silver and fine china. Instead of corncakes and pulque, the doctor eats sweet biscuits and drinks chocolate.

The subject of race, which had been a minor theme in *Of Mice and Men*, is of greater importance in *The Pearl*, where it is directly related to poverty and riches and the way an individual's worth is measured by society. For Kino and his family are Indians who have been beaten, starved, and robbed for almost four hundred years. In this story the Indians eke out an existence fishing for pearls to make others rich, or are servants of the rich, like the man who answers the doctor's door. Indians, we are told, are regarded as little more than animals, an observation reinforced by the doctor, who considers that "little Indians" ought to be treated by veterinarians.

By contrast, the doctor's white European race rules Mexico. Just as the king of Spain had risen to power by exploiting Mexico's wealth centuries ago, the doctor and his kind enjoy themselves at the expense of the Indians. The doctor's European identity is represented by his silk dressing gown from Paris and his continual fond memories of French restaurants, fine wine, and luxurious apartments.

Every facet of white Europeanized Mexican society wants the Indian race to remain in the station into which they were born and where they have suffered for four hundred years. For the Indian to try to rise in the world would be to risk bringing ruin on the whole community.

Every level of white society conspires to keep the Indian suppressed so he can be used to keep the others wealthy, whether they be the business community, represented by the pearl buyers, or those in the professions, represented by the doctor and the priest. The pearl buyers are really all agents of one powerful man who lives far away. They pretend to offer the Indians competitive prices for the pearls but are actually in league with one another, fixing prices to keep them low. It is a vicious system that cheats the Indians and keeps them in poverty.

Likewise, we see that the doctor cheats them, refusing at first to treat Coyotito at all, then using his superior knowledge to make

The very wealthy in Mexico in the nineteenth century: the San Gabriel hacienda.

The very poor in Mexico in the nineteenth century: native huts.

the baby sick again so that he can pretend to heal him, and finally sneaking back into the shack to steal the valuable pearl.

The priest and the church he represents are little better. While the doctor treats the poor like animals, the priest treats them like children. To those with money the church is generous, in the doctor's case allowing him to buy his dead wife's way into heaven. By contrast, the church refuses the poor Indians the simple rites of marriage and baptism. Kino and Juana have never had the money to pay the priest to marry them or to baptize their son. The priest acknowledges that now that they have the pearl, they can pay to be married. In the presence of both the doctor and the priest, Kino hears the Song of Evil.

The discovery of the valuable pearl causes Kino to realize that he and his neighbors have been cheated all their lives. A society motivated solely by greed destroys his boat (which he needs to make a living), burns his house, attacks him physically, hunts him and his wife down like animals, and kills his son.

Yet despite centuries of oppression, Kino can still hope for all those things considered to be part of the American Dream: decent clothes, the proper tools to make a living, the respectability that comes with the blessing of the church, and, above all, an education for his son—a way out of ignorance for the whole family.

In the particular ways in which *The Pearl* concentrates on class and race injustice, it is a reflection of the social history of Mexico. Spain acquired Mexico through conquest in the sixteenth century and continued to control it politically for four hundred years, so Spanish culture determined the course of life in Mexico, specifically the chasm between the very rich and the very poor and the inability of democracy to gain a foothold there as it did in the United States. Rulers in Spain remained absolute dictators who were unwilling to share their power with the people. In Mexico, as in Spain, there was for centuries no middle class—only the pure European, propertied upper class and a dirt poor Indian peasant class, much as one sees in *The Pearl*. The extent of resistance to democracy in Mexico in the eighteenth century can be seen in the actions of the church, which supported European government in Mexico; it even forbade the reading of the Declaration of Independence and the Constitution of the United States.

As the nineteenth century wore on, other social classes developed in Mexico, but lines between classes remained rigid, and few

Mexicans had enough freedom of movement to rise to a better life. There were still the *hacendados*, the powerful pure Europeans who owned most of the land in the country; there were the *Criollos*, who were born in Mexico rather than Europe, of mixed blood, and formed the professional ranks. There were the *Mestigos*, or small ranch owners. And at the bottom of the social ladder were the native American Indians. In a very real sense, "Mexican" was not a valid designation in that the country was completely divided into castes or rigid social groupings that had nothing to do with one another.

The European upper-class monopoly on power and money was such that even as late as the nineteenth century the poor were forbidden by law to grow cash crops, and the little land owned by Indians and small farmers was being confiscated.

In 1810 the first of many revolutions occurred in Mexico to break the monopoly of the upper class on land ownership and to bring some promise of a better life to people like Kino in *The Pearl*. One of the most famous of these many revolutionaries was a parish priest named Miguel Hidalgo who called the countryside to arms. Though Hidalgo attracted thousands of Mexicans to his cause and managed to capture several major townships, the Spanish had military superiority; ultimately the revolution failed, ending in the arrest and execution of those involved.

In 1812 another major revolution got under way under the leadership of a man named Morelos, also a parish priest and a former follower of Hidalgo. Morelos captured most of Mexico for a time. And the reforms he advocated were truly revolutionary: the establishment of democracy and equality, which would have necessitated a redistribution of land and wealth. But these reforms were too extreme for many of the *Criollos*, and the Spanish royalists were able to win back most of the territory that Morelos had gained. He himself was captured and executed in December 1815.

In 1821 a less extreme revolution under the leadership of Vicente Guerrero ousted General Agustin de Iturbide. Guerrero and his followers pushed for independence from Spain rather than for social reforms, and on September 27, 1821, the Spanish viceroy, who ruled Mexico in the name of the Spanish king, was driven out. Though Mexico now had political independence from Spain, the caste system remained strongly in place throughout the century, and the land and commerce in the country were still under the

control of aristocrats and Europeans. Priests born in Spain dominated the church, and officials born in Spain dominated public
policies. By the mid-nineteenth century, commerce throughout the
country, including the mines and farms, was in ruins. Although
Indians constituted between 30 and 40 percent of Mexico's population, they still had no political power and suffered from disease
and debt. They were virtual slaves in Mexico. Indians were
therefore interested chiefly in self-government, a fair distribution
of land, and the preservation of their own culture.

Mexico was no longer ruled by a Spanish viceroy, but by the
mid-nineteenth century, other foreign powers in search of the
great wealth to be had in Mexico's natural resources had virtually
colonized the country.

Into this situation in the 1850s came an Indian reformer, Benito
Juarez, who had miraculously risen to a political appointment. In
1867 he was confirmed as the reform leader of the country. However, Juarez and his supporters were able to do little more than
make political reforms, failing to touch social issues. The upper
class became more powerful than ever before, and foreign capital
increased more than it ever had before. The extent to which the
lower classes remained powerless can be seen in the educational
system of Mexico—a system to which Kino hopes he can buy access
for his son. Outside of the cities there were no schools of any kind.
Church schools had been closed, and with the exception of a few
costly private academies there was no way for a Mexican child to
receive an education in the country. Although Juarez and the re-
formers were committed to providing basic education to every
Mexican citizen, they fell far short of their goal. It is estimated that
even under educational reform, only 300,000 out of 9 million Mexicans received even the most basic education.

After another period of revolution following the death of Juarez,
Porfirio Díaz, one of the longest-lived leaders of Mexico, assumed
the presidency in 1876. He stepped down in 1880, reassumed the
presidency in 1884, and continued in office until 1911. Under
Diaz' rule, the taking of what were claimed to be "unused" lands
from Indians greatly speeded up, and further small ranches were
taken from the *Mestigo* peasants. Europeans and European immi-
grants acquired one-half of the land in Mexico and one-half of the
liquid wealth. Much of the land rich in minerals or with agricultural
potential was controlled by foreign corporations. Along with this

went a systematic attempt to destroy many of the peaceable agricultural Indian tribes like the Maya and the Yaquis. In his history
of Mexico entitled *Fire and Blood*, T. R. Fehrenbach describes the
situation as it existed in the first decade of the twentieth century:

> By the end of the century, at least half of the territory of the Re-
> public belonged to a few thousand families and foreign operators.
> More than half of the cropland was divided between not more than
> ten thousand haciendas or *latifundios*. It has been estimated that
> about one million families had been dispossessed of their land and
> reduced to vagabondage or peonage. Only three percent of the rural
> families owned any farmland.
>
> • • •
>
> Human labor was so cheap in the oversupply that it cost less to hire
> a man than to rent a mule.
>
> • • •
>
> The average peon or working man remained eternally in debt, either
> to his patron or to the hacienda store which supplied him with
> necessities. Under the law these debts were passed on from father
> to son. On some estates, especially the foreign-owned plantations,
> there was a new form of wage: the hacienda ticket or token, ex-
> changeable only at the company store.[1]

By 1910 the poorer Mexicans had reached the lowest possible standard of living. Having been stripped of their land, they were no
longer able to produce sufficient food for their own survival, and
their lives were characterized by despair and alcoholism.

The situation in Mexico at this time produced the longest and
bloodiest of its many revolutions and the most famous of its revolutionaries, including, in the north, the bandit-revolutionary Pan-
cho Villa, and, in the area called Morelos, the leader of small
farmers and Indians, Emiliano Zapata. In Morelos, thirty powerful
families had taken all the lands owned by small farmers and all the
lands of the Indians. Zapata, who had been an activist for many
years, began organizing an army in the south to fight for a more
just distribution of land to the poor. To this end, he and his followers sacked and burned the wealthy haciendas in their path,
contributing mightily to the overthrow of the old Diaz government
in 1911 and to the establishment of a new constitution. Zapata and

Villa met to formulate the new constitution, but Zapata refused to lay down his arms until the new government promised land reforms and the immediate confiscation of large plantations. Thus the revolution went on as various personalities with differing philosophies warred with one another. Finally, in 1919, Zapata was tricked and led into an ambush where he was killed. At about the same time that Steinbeck was revising *The Pearl* for film presentation, he was also writing what would be one of his most successful screenplays, that for the film *Viva Zapata!*, which chronicled the life of the famous revolutionary.

The documents that follow are arranged chronologically and present first-hand observations made between 1901 and 1923. One can observe those conditions characteristic of Mexico that add texture to Steinbeck's story about a poor Indian peasant and his wife and child. Excerpts from *A Glimpse of Old Mexico* present a sympathetic view of the poor, who are hampered by a rigid social structure based on race. Those from *An American Girl in Mexico* paint an equally sympathetic portrait of the lives of hard-working peasants exploited by the aristocrats and the clergy. *On the Mexican Highlands* (1906) was written specifically about the central place of *pulque* in the lives of lower-class Mexicans. The excerpts from *Mexico with Comparisons and Conclusions* (1907) give an account of sanitary and health conditions among the poor. The excerpts from *Mexico as I Saw It* (1911) describe the work, religion, and home life of the Mexican laborer. Passages from *The Real Mexico* (1914) explain the skewed system of justice in the country, whereby the wealthy have secured more and more land and the peasants have been displaced. Finally, excerpts from *The Social Revolution in Mexico* deal with the failure of education in the country.

JAMES H. WILKINS' *A GLIMPSE OF OLD MEXICO*

[T]he hundreds of years of subjugation were cut deep in him.
The Pearl, 30

Familiarity with Mexico's rigid caste system, based in large measure on matters of race—the native Indians at the bottom and the white Europeans at the top—is essential to an understanding of *The Pearl*, which refers repeatedly to the great separation between the two groups. Firsthand observations of this social system were made by "a tenderfoot editor," James H. Wilkins, when he toured Mexico in 1901. According to Wilkins, the fortunes of the wealthy are usually made on the backs of impoverished workers, and these masses of poor people the world over supply the labor and the creativity that make or break a nation.

Note in the following passages his references to early conquest of the Mexican Indians by the Spanish, a conquest that is repeated daily in the lives of Kino and the natives that Wilkins observes. Note also Wilkins' belief that the business communities of Mexico and foreign countries that do business in Mexico prey on the powerless workers. Even the church, which supports the wealthy aristocrats, withholds the sacrament of marriage from those who cannot pay.

FROM JAMES H. WILKINS, *A GLIMPSE OF OLD MEXICO* (1901)

In the great mass of Mexican people, the Indian stock predominates. I should say that at least three-quarters of their ancestry could be traced back to the aboriginal populations of the country. But it must be remembered, in the first place, that the Mexican Indians were of a far higher type intellectually than the nomads of the north, that they had a written language, had solved many astronomical problems, were expert builders, had a regularly organized government and in short, had traveled far on the road to a high civilization. How sturdy the stock was, is best illustrated by the fact that their descendants are here today. Following the Spanish conquest, . . . the natives had been . . . assigned to the various conquerors who happened to have a pull. Then they were duly branded on the cheek to locate their ownership and became chattels of masters who exercised over them the absolute right of life or death. The greater number of them were sent to work in the mines, the remainder being employed to raise corn for their food and to pack it into the mountains. The miners passed practically their whole lives in the damp underground workings, to prevent attempts to escape. I have seen in an old mine the niches cut in the rock walls, where they slept. It was as rigorous a form of slavery as ever existed and in most parts of the Americas the native races crumbled under it to dust. . . . The Mexican slaves alone survived and when freedom came at length early in the present century, they were if anything more numerous than when Cortez and his followers landed in their country. So, physically, at least, they must have possessed the rugged type that goes with a survival of the fittest.

Even when liberty was given them, it seemed as though they had gained nothing by the change. Under their Spanish masters, they had at least some protection from outside foes, just as any valuable chattel is guarded. During the stormy half century succeeding Mexican independence even this was withdrawn. In that distracted period, with revolutions occurring every few months and the country swarming with freebooters, outlaws and desperadoes, the helpless people suffered even more severely than in the days of bondage, for the population of Mexico decreased rapidly, the loss being estimated variously at from two to five millions.

And in their contact with European civilization, the native races acquired nothing worthy of mention. . . . Not the slightest effort was made to educate them and it is perfectly safe to say that twenty-five years ago not one in a thousand was able to read or write. In no sense was their condition improved. Cortez found the native races clad in cotton fabrics and cotton is the dress of the lower orders to this day. . . . Even their food has been modified very slightly. The native beans, or frijolis, tortillas or baked fruits, are the great staples they were four hundred years ago and are prepared for consumption the same way.

• • •

If you wish to hire a man who has been out of employment for a few days, it is almost certainty that you will have to redeem his raiment in order to enable him to make an appearance in public. Their recklessness and necessities are preyed upon by a swarm of pawnbrokers, about as conscienceless a crew of pirates as can be found the world over. When you find a genuine shark among a people given to free-handedness, the chances are that he will go the limit and something more. This is particularly true of the Mexican pawnbrokers, who are absolutely without pity or remorse. I have watched their hard, cruel, merciless faces as they worked some unhappy peon to a finish.

• • •

Ceremonial marriage among the peons is the exception, not the rule. Two marriages, if any, are usually performed[,] the civil and ecclesiastical, and as both mean fees, the thrifty people usually prefer to celebrate their nuptials by having a good time, instead of squandering money on priests and magistrates. There are about forty families at our mine and in only two cases are the heads joined in lawful wedlock. The balance have simply elected to live together in the condition of husband and wife without further form than mutual consent. I know that some of my readers will cry out in horror at the statement and wish never to hear of a Mexican again. But, on the other hand this free and easy relation is maintained in a majority of instances, with a good deal of fidelity, as a rule to the close of life.

San Rafael, Calif., pp. 33–43.

ELIZABETH VISERE MCGARY'S *AN AMERICAN GIRL IN MEXICO*

> This doctor was of a race which for nearly four hundred years
> had beaten and starved and robbed and despised Kino's race.
>
> *The Pearl*, 9

A 1904 account of Mexico by "an American girl," Elizabeth Visere McGary, expresses sentiments toward the working-class Mexican similar to those of Wilkins, noting the injustices that come from the vast differences between the haves and the have-nots in the first decade of the nineteenth century.

McGary could well be describing the contrasts between the household of the doctor in *The Pearl* and that of Kino. She also comments on the place of the church in the oppression of the poor.

FROM ELIZABETH VISERE MCGARY, *AN AMERICAN GIRL IN MEXICO* (1904)

Senor Carlos seldom came in until ten, when she [the servant called Luz] would prepare a fresh meal for him. But a happier soul than Luz it would be hard to find. The boy who answered the bell was her son, a dwarfed creature of sixteen, with a solemn face many years too old for the little body. If one could have a dollar for every step Pedro took during the day, pacing back and forth with *tortillas*, that person would be rich indeed, yet he received only two dollars and fifty cents a month, Mexican money, for all that work. When one sees these conditions—sees faithful sewing girls work twelve hours a day for twenty-five cents, Mexican money, and only skilled hands receive more, eating their dinner with the servants, and being in every way treated without consideration, the heart is filled with pity.

In a household of affluence there is hardly a limit to the number of servants. At least in a pretentious home may always be found a *portero* (doorkeeper), *cochero* (coachman), *recamerera* (chambermaid), *lavandera* (laundress), *planchadora* (ironing woman), *caballerango* (hostler), *mozo* (runner of all errands), *cocinera* (cook), *molendera* (woman who grinds corn), and most pompous of all, the *lacayo*, or footman. Families leading a more modest existence endure the hardships of having but five or six servants. A lady never summons her help except by slapping the hands quickly together; this method is also used in the streets for calling an inferior.

• • •

The *peons* subsist entirely on the clammy cold *tortillas* and the native boiled *frijole* beans, enough of which can be bought for a few pennies to feed a family all day. No housekeeper furnishes her servants any other food than this. Perhaps this is the reason that Pedro, who carried *tortillas*, answered the bell, aroused the household and announced meals, presented what seemed to me such an old, unsmiling face for a child.

• • •

The Cathedral is magnificent, but the recent substitution of wooden floors for tiling detracts greatly from its beauty. There is no telling the money that has been spent on that building, and in it. The jeweled crown on the Virgin Mary cost thousands of dollars—paid for chiefly by the hordes of poor who worship there.

New York: Dodd, Mead and Co., pp. 22–146.

WILLIAM SEYMOUR EDWARDS' *ON THE MEXICAN HIGHLANDS*

And he drank a little pulque and that was breakfast.

The Pearl, 4

Several times in *The Pearl* mention is made of the *pulque* which Kino drinks at different times during the day. This alcoholic concoction was used by the Indians as a means of psychologically escaping the reality of their hard lives of suffering, which held little comfort or hope.

Professional travel writer William Seymour Edwards explains in this 1906 account the pervasiveness of this intoxicant in Mexican society—how it is made, how it is used, and how it affects both individuals and society.

FROM WILLIAM SEYMOUR EDWARDS, *ON THE MEXICAN HIGHLANDS* (1906)

Mexico City, I think, may be said to be enwrapped with the scent of *pulque* (*Pool-Kay*). "*Pulque*, blessed *pulque*," says the Mexican! *Pulque*, the great national drink of the ancient Aztec, which has been readily adopted by the Spanish conqueror, and which is to-day the favorite intoxicating beverage of every bibulating Mexican. At the railway stations, as we descended into the great valley wherein Mexico City lies, Indian women handed up little brown pitchers of *pulque*, fresh *pulque* new tapped. Sweet and cool and delicious it was, as mild as lemonade (in this unfermented condition it is called *agua miel*, honey water. . . . Through miles and miles we traversed plantations of the maguey plant from which the *pulque* is extracted. For *pulque* is merely the sap of the maguey or "century plant," which accumulates at the base of the flower stalk, just before it begins to shoot up. The *pulque* gatherer thrusts a long, hollow reed into the stalk, sucks it full to the mouth, using the tongue for a stopper, and then blows it into a pigskin sack which he carries on his back. When the pigskin is full of juice, it is emptied into a tub, and when the tub is filled with liquor it is poured into a cask, and the cask is shipped to the nearest market. Itinerant pedlars tramp through the towns and villages, bearing a pigskin of *pulque* on their shoulders and selling drinks to whosoever is thirsty and may have the *uno centavo* (one cent) to pay for it. When fresh, the drink is delightful and innocuous. But when the liquid has begun to ferment, it is said to generate narcotic qualities which make it the finest thing for a steady, long-continuing and thorough-going drunk which Providence has yet put within the reach of man. Thousands of gallons of *pulque* are consumed in Mexico City every twenty-four hours, and the government has enacted stringent laws providing against the sale of *pulque* which shall be more than twenty-four hours old. The older it grows the greater the drunk, and the less you need drink to become intoxicated, hence, it is the aim of every thirsty Mexican to procure the oldest *pulque* he can get. In every pulque shop, where only the mild, sweet *agua miel*, fresh and innocuous, is supposed to be sold, there is, as a matter of fact, always on hand a well fermented supply, a few nips of which will knock out the most confirmed drinker almost as soon as he can swallow it.

Cincinnati: Press of Jennings and Graham, pp. 70–72.

A. A. GRAHAM'S *MEXICO WITH COMPARISONS AND CONCLUSIONS*

"Have you money to pay for the treatment?"

The Pearl, 11

Much of *The Pearl* has to do with the sad state of the Indians' nutrition and health, especially that of the child Coyotito, and the inhumane behavior of one person—the doctor—to whom they must turn for help.

In *Mexico* (1907), A. A. Graham, an attorney from Kansas, published his observations on the illnesses and malnutrition of Mexico's poor. The death rate is high, he observes, coming chiefly from smallpox and starvation.

FROM A. A. GRAHAM, *MEXICO WITH COMPARISONS AND CONCLUSIONS* (1907)

Following smallpox, I place death from starvation in which I will include all those deteriorating influences due to lack of proper clothing and properly warmed and ventilated shelter. The poor people of Mexico, and that means about ninety-five percent of them, live on the ground. Now, call over the acts of eating, sleeping, working, resting, and you have it, if you do not comprehend the full force of the statement that they live on the ground. They have simply appropriated a spot of earth around which, on the plateaus, they have built mud or stone walls, sometimes not as compact as a stone fence, usually with earthen roof; and in the tierra caliente, or hot country, have walled themselves in with a stockade of sticks, cornstalks or sugarcane, but sometimes with rushes, with roofs usually of grasses. On the plateaus, where the climate is inhospitable, and, sometimes, severe, people have no fuel for heating purposes, but only a small amount of sticks, cornstalks, or such like, for cooking after the most primitive forms.

For clothing, they have one layer of a thin cotton cloth, and always a blanket, which serves as a wrap during the day and a bed at night. Folding themselves in this blanket, they lie down on the ground, or sit up against the wall, and sleep. Barefoot always, with the exception of the men who wear sandals of their own make, consisting of a piece of common sole leather, attached to the foot with straps.

In the terribly big hat, the sombrero, is where we strike their extravagance, but most of them, however, can only afford poor and cheap ones.

Their food is never sufficient to sustain life properly, and is often down to a sort of siege basis, so that they lack full growth and proper development; and the starvation, in the large sense in which I have employed the term, is of slow progress. Those who survive infancy and youth, with this insufficient and bad diet, frequently dry up, become mummified, in their old age. I have seen many old people of no perceptible frame except skin and bone, apparent mummies, presenting the most dejected and pitiable sight imaginable; but no state, however deplorable, has ever been too lamentable not to be the object of man's levity; and people say that these poor wretches are walking around to save funeral expenses.

• • •

In infancy and in youth, the number of deaths due to lack of nourishment, if starvation seems too strong a term, is simply appalling. Think of an undertaker having, as his sign, a little coffin, swinging from a string over his door! This is the usual sign in Mexico.

Topeka, Kans.: Crane and Co., pp. 254–257.

MRS. ALEC TWEEDIE'S *MEXICO AS I SAW IT*

[T]hey were being married now that they could pay.

The Pearl, 24

One of the most widely traveled visitors to Mexico, Mrs. Alec Tweedie wrote several books on the subject in the second decade of the twentieth century. Although she was friendly with wealthy and powerful Mexicans and a frequent visitor in their homes, Mrs. Tweedie was also appalled at the living and working conditions of the poor, making reference to laborers in mines and factories and on ranches. She also contrasts the poverty of the Indians with the ostentatious wealth of the churches.

FROM MRS. ALEC TWEEDIE, *MEXICO AS I SAW IT* (1911)

The days of slavery are over; nevertheless on many of the native Mexican ranches there are still "peons," who are so bound that they cannot get away, and if they try to escape the master sends for them, and generally manages to evade the law, and insists on their return. The following facts show to what magnitude the "peon system" has grown. On one ranch in San Luis, where about a thousand persons are employed, the total debt of the peons amounts to one hundred and twenty thousand dollars. Anyone buying a ranch of this sort is obliged to purchase the peons' debt, which practically means buying them as slaves. The law while prohibiting this system, practically encourages it. . . . To my personal knowledge, the saddest of lives are being dragged out on some of those ranches.

• • •

The men working in some of the large factories live in hovels built of bamboo reeds, which are often so small and low that a man cannot stand upright in his own home. They look like gipsy tents, and yet the tenants are content to live in them year after year. A thatch of palm leaves lets in the rain, bamboo walls admit the wind, and the floor is mother earth. If a man possess a pig he is considered wealthy, and that pig shares his home. If he has a bed he is much to be envied, for old sacks thrown on the bare ground form the Indian's usual couch. In the middle of the hut—which probably measures twelve feet by eight—is his cooking stove, made by placing two or three bricks on the ground, and the smoke issuing therefrom finds its way out between the palm leaves, which in the same manner let the rain in.

The family possessions consist of a square tin can—which originally held oil—and is universally used for hot water, or for washing the clothes of the family or even for cooking in a large way. There is always a stone trough on four legs—*metate*—so named for the lava rock of which it is made, and this is used for grinding the Indian corn which the housewife makes into *tortillas*. She sits on her heels in true native fashion, and rubs a small roller up and down until she has ground the corn. This, with water, she makes into dough, takes a small quantity in her hand, pats it out flat until it is the size of a plate and very thin, then she puts it into an iron pan and bakes it over the fire, thus preparing the staple food of the family.

• • •

They cannot read or write, they do not know how to think; all they want is food and shelter, and so their animal existence continues year in, year out.

• • •

With the rich folk marriage is the natural sequence [of courtship], and all goes well, or ought to.

With the poor folk it is otherwise. Enquiries have lately been set on foot concerning the morality of village life, and the consequent discoveries are positively appalling. There are pueblos where no wedding has occurred in a generation!

• • •

The Cathedral is a handsome edifice. It represents wealth and splendour. The massive balustrades are of solid silver; the candelabra hanging from the ceiling are beautiful, and on this occasion some thousands of candles shed a lurid glow on all around. The priests in gorgeous robes, the decorations of flowers and palms, the quantities of incense giving cloud-like mysticism to the scene, told of wealth unbounded, while kneeling upon the stone flags in various stages of poverty and abject rags were the Indians. Oh, how poor they were!

• • •

It was certainly a wonderful sight; the enthusiasm of these people was extraordinary. Rags and religion were on every side.

• • •

There are many rich people, millionaires in fact, who live in veritable palaces. The homes of the two Escandon families, situated on each side of the Jockey Club, are simply splendid; patio after patio, stabling for twenty or thirty horses downstairs, suites and suites of apartments. The numbers of servants kept by these old Mexican families is surprising, forty or fifty for one household. Many of these servants have been in the family all their lives, and their parents before them; but the Mexican servant, though faithful, is lazy, and two only get through the same amount of work as one ordinary European.

The country houses also are wonderful—often old monasteries changed into sumptuous mansions. They contain corridors, patios and cloisters in abundance, and such flowers. Hardly in gardens, for the lovely blooms practically grow wild, only grass borders, lawns and roadways requiring attention.

New York: Thomas Nelson and Sons, pp. 60–246.

H. HAMILTON FYFE'S *THE REAL MEXICO*

The political situation in Mexico is the subject of a 1914 book, *The Real Mexico*, by H. Hamilton Fyfe, whose interests in his many travels included the workings of countries undergoing turmoil and reform.

Fyfe concentrates on the political and economic injustices, like those under which Kino labors, and which have led to the country's upheaval. He mentions in particular the exploitation of the poor by the church and the Catholic Party and the need for land reform.

FROM H. HAMILTON FYFE, *THE REAL MEXICO* (1914)

Mexico in one respect resemble[s] France before the Revolution. Almost all the land is held by rich men who manage to escape taxes. Porfirio Diaz was called a strong man, yet he was afraid to reform this abuse. He failed lamentably also in permitting the landowners to practise criminal extortion and fraud. The "peons" (peasants) have in many parts been deprived of their holding[s], either by being cheated out of them, or by being loaded with chains of debt. Here is an example of the tricks played upon the unlettered Indian. An edict was issued that land in certain parts must be registered by a certain date. Many Indians were kept in ignorance of that order. Unregistered land was put up for sale, and in some cases bought at ridiculously low prices. Protesting, but unable to resist the injustice, the wretched owners were dispossessed. Nor was that all. After losing their property, they often became slaves.

Thousands of peasants are in bondage to their employers—the great "Hacendados." They are obliged to buy at the "Hacienda" store. Credit is easy. In time, the employers have an account against them which they can never hope to pay. Or else they borrow in order to be married. Church fees are heavy, but the Mexican peasant feels "more married" if the knot is tied by a priest, and the women are good Catholics. Or it may be that funds are wanted for a funeral and "wake." Somehow or other the thoughtless peon gives his employer a hold over him. His mortgaged land is taken, and so long as he owes money he cannot go away. Worse still, the debt descends to his children.

The condition of these peons is practically that of slaves. Yet slavery is a word which sounds worse than the condition for which it stands. There are harsh "Hacendados," just as there were some Simon Legrees, but as a rule the peasants are decently treated. If they were not, they would not go back at regular intervals to their "haciendas" when they are working in mines. It is said that "if you want to catch a peon and pay off a score, all you need do is to go and sit on his 'tierra' " (that is, the district where he was born). He is certain, sooner or later, to go back to it. This love of the land on which they were raised is one of the strongest passions in Mexican hearts.

The Indians usually cultivate their patches on a profit-sharing basis. Half goes to the owner, half to them. Or else the peasant is given a patch to cultivate for himself while he works on his master's land. The owners put under tillage only a very small part of their enormous properties, which in some cases, as in that of the Terrazas family in Chihuahua, extend over hundreds of miles.

• • •

Land reform is, therefor[e], a necessity in Mexico. But it is not advocated by the Constitutionalists only. Men of good will and foresight on the other side are equally convinced that it must come. Even Senor Limantour, one of the Ministers who brought about the downfall of Porfirio Diaz, admitted that the huge estates had to be broken up, and also that judicial and municipal abuses must be swept away.

One of the hardships which the poor are beginning to resent is forced labour on public works. In a certain town a new building was required for the local archives. Money was voted for its erection, but the money was not all devoted to that purpose. "Peon" labourers were arrested upon some trifling or trumped-up charge and compelled to dig the foundations.

• • •

Nothing is said by the Catholic Party's programme about a change in voting qualifications. That can easily be understood. It is the Catholic Party which stands to profit by priestly exploitation of the peon.

• • •

In the Catholic Party there are a number of men whose talent is above the average and who in sincerity of purpose also rank high. But there is none who stands out with the mark of a leader upon him. Most of the chiefs of the party are large landowners, and they take, as is natural, the landowner's point of view. They say nothing about the injustice of exempting the huge estates from taxation. They would no doubt oppose even a tax upon uncultivated land, which would help to break up these properties. Their ideal of government for Mexico is an enlightened paternalism, which, could it but be realized, and did it wisely share its power with the new middle class, would ideally meet the case. But in that qualification "enlightened" the difficulty lies.

• • •

"If you gave him land," said one of the most prominent Catholic Party chiefs when we were discussing this, "he would only sell it and then complain that the buyer had robbed him of it." In which there is, as all who have studied the peon will testify, a large element of truth. But this must be recollected, too—that the *jefes politicos* [career politicians] manage the elections and secure the victory of the candidate whom they are instructed by the President through the Governors of states to return. Therefore they stand in the Catholic Party's way. Since honest elections would enormously benefit that party, "Honest elections" is their chief cry.

• • •

It is the absence of a sound basis in education which makes the real Mexicans like children; bright up to a point, pleasant mannered, easy to get on with, kindly, unassuming, and apparently European; but without understanding of the apparatus of civilization which they have borrowed ready-made, and utterly unable to appreciate the European point of view. Those who deal with them successfully treat them as children.

New York: McBride, Nast and Co., pp. 65–189.

EDWARD ALSWORTH ROSS' *THE SOCIAL REVOLUTION IN MEXICO*

"My son will go to school," [Kino] said.

The Pearl, 25

Kino's first aspiration upon finding the precious pearl is to provide his son with an education, not only so that Coyotito can have a better life, but also so that the educated son can dispel his father's ignorance—so that Kino can know what is true and what is not, for all those with greater knowledge—from the doctor to the pearl buyers—have cheated and deceived Kino's people for centuries.

Edward Alsworth Ross, a sociology professor, investigated the country's system of education and speculated about its importance to its humbler citizens who, like Kino, have never had learning available to them.

Ross begins with an interview of Mexico's president, Porfirio Díaz.

FROM EDWARD ALSWORTH ROSS, *THE SOCIAL REVOLUTION IN MEXICO* (1923)

"Why, then, Mr. President, don't you educate your people faster?"

"Ah, my friend, I am not all-powerful as many people imagine. On the one hand, the *hacendados* oppose popular education lest the peon should want more and ask more wages. On the other hand, the church is hostile to it, and even in my own family I meet opposition."

Senora Diaz, as is well known, was under clerical influence and did her utmost to shape her husband's policies to the advantage of the church.

In any case, Diaz did not take up education early enough nor heartily enough. If only he had pushed enlightenment with any thing like the energy with which he pushed material development! In the embellishment of the capital he lavished sums which, had they been expended in dispelling the cloud of ignorance which hung over the land, might have averted the social explosion that shattered his painfully wrought fabric.

• • •

... [O]ld Bourbon aristocrats told me that Diaz's fatal mistake was in not leaving education entirely to the church. "State schools can never train the masses to keep their place," insisted a great landowner, angered because some of his acres were being taken to create *ejidos* [public institutions]. "Only the church can instil the motives which will make the childlike, ignorant peons truthful, obedient, and regardful of the rights of property-owners."

• • •

The revolutionary leaders have quite broken with the aristocratic ideal of education as the prerogative of the children of the more fortunate classes and with the church's ideal of education as an opiate to make the masses insensible to the hopelessness of their lot. They accept, without reserve, the democratic ideal of education for "all the children of all the people."

• • •

The hope is in their children. If you can reach them with the right kind of an education, you can fire them with ambition to live better than their parents and advance to a higher social plane. The beginning of the ascent of the masses waits on popular education, the one key to the regeneration of Mexico. Nothing else really matters.

New York: Century Co., pp. 152–155.

NOTE

1. T. R. Fehrenbach, *Fire and Blood* (New York: Collier Books, 1973), p. 465.

TOPICS FOR WRITTEN OR ORAL EXPLORATION

1. View the film *Viva Zapata!* Write an essay on its relationship to *The Pearl.*

2. Some critics argue that *The Pearl*'s message is devoid of politics. What do you think? Construct a convincing argument on either side of this question.

3. James H. Wilkins makes reference to slavery in the South in a discussion of Mexico. What parallels can you draw?

4. James H. Wilkins argues that many a millionaire's fortune has been made on the backs of the poor. Support or refute his statement with hard evidence from history.

5. Read a history of Native Americans in the United States and write an essay comparing their condition in the twentieth century with that of Mexican Indians in *The Pearl.*

6. Literacy and education have always been critical issues in the history of oppressed peoples. Note, for example, that it has been illegal in various societies to educate the poor. (It was illegal to teach slaves in the American South to read.) Do research on the laws or sentiments against allowing members of the populace to read in a given country at some particular time. What dangers did literacy pose to those in power? For argument's sake, stage a debate between someone who believes that educating the poor is dangerous and someone who, like Edward Ross, believes that the growth and well-being of a country depend on an educated populace.

7. Kino sees that educating his son will make the family less helpless. How would you present a full-fledged argument to someone thinking of dropping out of school that education is power?

8. For what reasons would a powerful church-supported government want to discourage marriage among the poor? Note that in slavery times in the United States, it was usually illegal for slaves to marry.

9. There is little discussion of land ownership in *The Pearl.* Nevertheless, the idea was a key one in the Mexican Revolution. After doing some reading on the subject, write a comparison of Native American attitudes toward the land as found in a history of Mexico and one of the United States.

10. Write an essay or have a debate on the question of whether Kino acted admirably. Should he have sold the pearl early on when he had a chance to do so or thrown it away as Juana thought he should?

SUGGESTIONS FOR FURTHER READING

Atkin, Ronald. *Revolution! Mexico, 1910–20*. New York: John Day, 1970.

Dunn, H. H. *The Crimson Jester*. New York: National Travel Club, 1934.

Fehrenbach, T. R. *Fire and Blood*. New York: Collier Books, 1973.

Lansing, Marion. *Liberators and Heroes of Mexico and Central America*. Boston: L. P. Page, 1941.

Ober, Frederick A. *Travels in Mexico*. Boston: Estes and Lauriate, 1885.

O'Hea, Patrick. *Reminiscences of the Mexican Revolution*. London: Sphere Books, 1981.

O'Shaughnessy, Edith. *Intimate Pages of Mexican History*. New York: George H. Doran, 1920.

Pinchon, Edgcumb. *Zapata, the Unconquerable*. New York: Doubleday, Doran, 1941.

Reed, John. *Insurgent Mexico*. New York: D. Appleton, 1914.

Index

About the Author

CLAUDIA DURST JOHNSON is Professor of English at the University of Alabama, where she chaired the Department of English for 12 years. She is series editor of the Greenwood Press "Literature in Context" series, which includes her works, *Understanding Adventures of Huckleberry Finn* (1996) and *Understanding The Scarlet Letter* (1995). She is also the author of *To Kill a Mockingbird: Threatening Boundaries* (1994), *The Productive Tension of Hawthorne's Art* (1981), and *American Actress: Perspectives on the Nineteenth Century* (1984), and coauthor (with Vernon Johnson) of *Memoirs of the Nineteenth-Century Theatre* (Greenwood, 1982), and (with Henry Jacobs) *An Annotated Bibliography of Shakespearean Burlesques, Parodies, and Travesties* (1976), as well as numerous articles on American literature and theatre.